365
AMAZING
FACTS

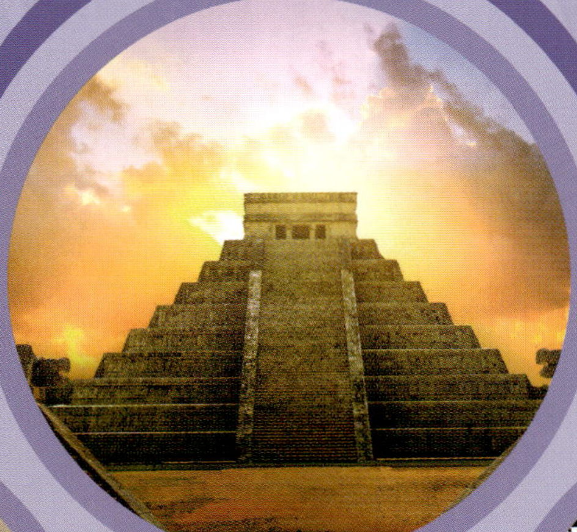

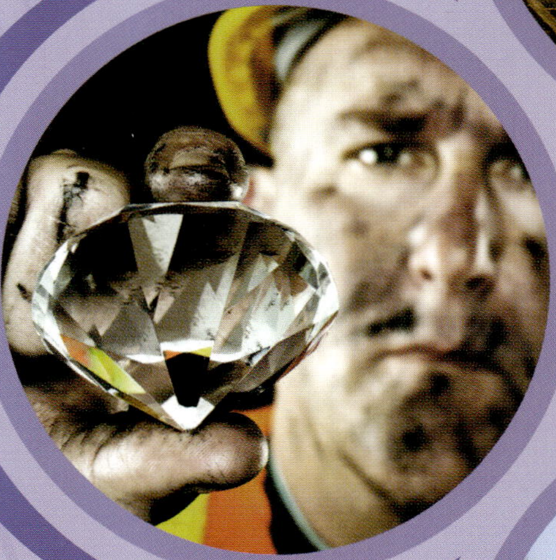

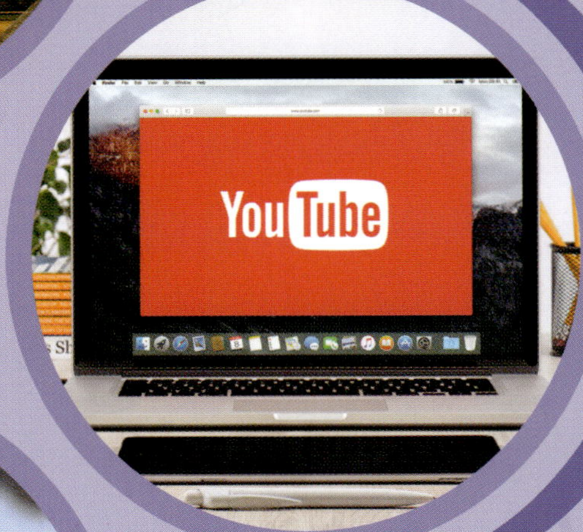

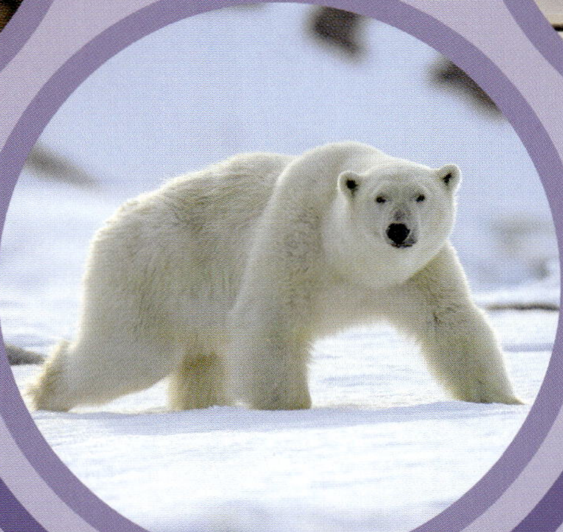

www.pegasusforkids.com

Published by Kuldeep Jain for B. Jain Publishers (P) Ltd., D-157, Sector 63, Noida - 201307, U.P
Registered office: 1921/10, Chuna Mandi, Paharganj, New Delhi-110055

Printed in India

Contents

1. Do you wonder why stars twinkle?

Actually stars don't twinkle at all. They only appear to twinkle. This is why it happens. The light of the stars reaches us by passing through the atmosphere of the Earth, which is made up of many layers of gases. These gases have different temperatures, pressures and several pockets of hot and cold air. When light passes through these gases, it gets slightly affected by these factors and bends a little this way and that. When we view this wavering light from the ground, it appears that the stars are twinkling.

Oh, wait! Is that why a coin on the floor of the swimming pool appears to be twinkling and dancing? It seems the light just can't stay in a straight line because of these distractions!

2. Why do stars only come out at night?

The stars are there in the sky both during the day and at night. During the day, the Sun shines so brightly that we cannot see the other stars present in the sky. At night, when the Sun goes down and the sky is dark, the light of the stars can be seen. Have you noticed how stars start to appear as the Sun starts to set? Do you know that the Sun is also a star? It shines brighter than the other stars as it is very close to the Earth while the other stars are far away.

3. What is a star? Why does it shine?

A star is a huge ball made of hot gases. The main gas in a star is hydrogen. The hydrogen atoms are constantly bumping into each other with so much force that it makes the hydrogen burn. This reaction produces lots of heat and light, which makes the star shine. When hydrogen atoms collide with each other to give out this light, another gas called helium is also produced in the process. So, a star is basically made up of two main gases; hydrogen and helium.

4. How far are the stars from Earth?

Stars are billions of kilometres away from each other. Yes, that sounds like an awesome distance. Isn't it? Since the stars are so far away, it takes a huge amount of time for the light of the star to reach us. Depending on the distance of the star from the Earth, the light of the star can take seconds, minutes and sometimes even years to reach us!

What does a light year mean? Let's find out.

5. What is a light year?

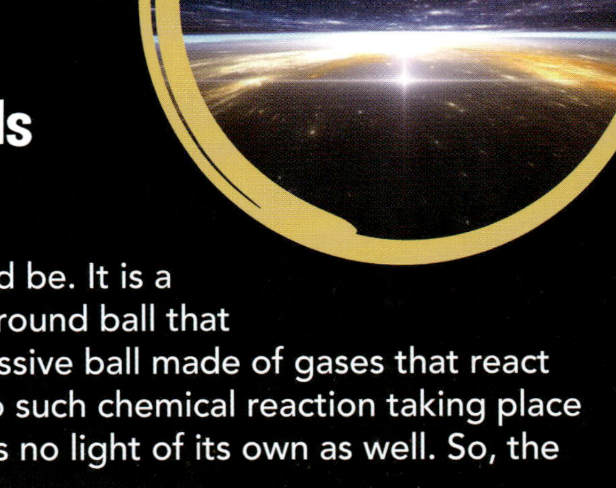

Light year is the distance that the light travels in one year. So, if we read somewhere that a star is 4 light-years away, we know what it means right? It means that it will take 4 years for the light of that star to reach us.

6. Sun is a star. What about Moon? Is Moon also a star?

No, Moon is not a star. Moon is not as big as a star should be. It is a natural satellite of the Planet Earth. A satellite is a small, round ball that revolves around a planet. As we now know, a star is a massive ball made of gases that react with each other to give out heat and light. But there is no such chemical reaction taking place on the Moon. Since it doesn't burn any hydrogen, there is no light of its own as well. So, the Moon doesn't qualify to be a star!

7. Do you know many other planets have their own moons as well?

In fact, some planets have more than one moon. For example, Jupiter has 67 moons, Saturn has 62 moons, Uranus has 27 moons and Neptune has 13 moons. Mercury and Venus have no moons at all. What is more interesting is that this number keeps on changing. As scientists continue their research and studies on space, they keep finding a new information and new facts. For example, some years back we only knew that Jupiter has 63 moons until scientists found out more as they explored the universe further with new technologies. Pretty amazing, isn't it?

8. If there is no reaction of gases on the Moon, why does the Moon shine? Where does the light come from?

Moon is actually very dark with no light of its own. It is basically a big mirror that reflects the Sun's light. It is the light of the Sun that makes it shine.

Do you know how far the Moon is from the Earth? The Moon is roughly 1.27 light seconds from the Earth. It means the light from the Moon takes 1.27 light seconds to reach us. Let's see what this distance means if we travel by car. It would take approximately 130 days to reach the Moon by car but cars don't go in space! If you, however, travel by rocket, it would take 13 hours to reach the Moon.

9. Why does the Moon change shapes every day?

Moon rotates around the Earth in a kind of circle called orbit. As we know, it is Sun's light that illuminates the Moon. Now, the Sun always lights up only one side of the Moon. So, we would see only the part that is lit by sunlight. Since the Moon is always changing its position and is never at the same place, different sides are illuminated in different ways on different days. As we see only the part that is illuminated, the shape appears to change every time the Moon changes its position. But it happens very slowly as the speed at which Moon orbits around the Earth is not super fast!

10. Earth is round. If this is true why don't we slip off and fly away in the space?

We live on Planet Earth. Earth has a force or power that pulls objects towards it. This force is called gravity. It is the gravity that keeps us on Earth and keep us from flying away into space. In fact, every object - big or small that has some mass, pulls the other with this force called gravity. The mass of the Earth and the mass of our body attract each other. But the mass of the Earth is greater and that is why the force with which it pulls us is stronger. This is the reason we never fly off into space!

Sir Isaac Newton discovered gravity when he wondered about why an apple fell on the ground rather than flying away. So, is gravity working only when something is falling? No, gravity is always pulling down on us even when we are sitting or standing still.

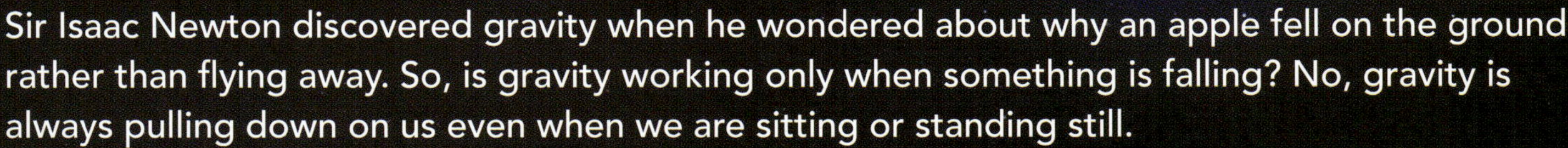

11. Gravity is the reason why Earth and other planets revolve around the Sun and why Moon revolves around the Earth. Are you wondering how?

Let's find out. Earth and Moon pull each other with some gravitational force. It is like a game of tug-of-war. Now, Moon is smaller than the Earth so it doesn't have enough strength to pull away completely but it is not so weak either to just snap and lose the game. So, this game keeps going on and the Moon keeps revolving around the Earth in an orbit.

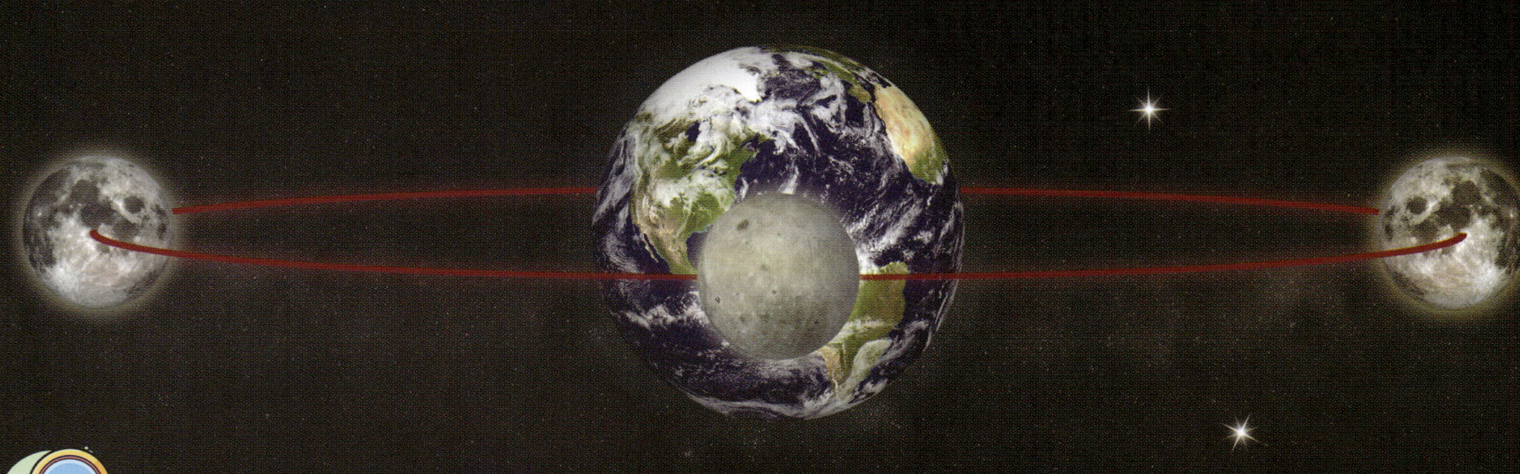

12. Has anyone been on the Moon?

For many years, America and Russia were trying to land on the Moon. An American astronaut Neil Armstrong made that dream come true as he became the first person in history to walk on the Moon. He, along with Buzz Aldrin, landed on the moon in his spacecraft called Apollo11 on July 16, 1969. The whole world tuned to watch this historic moment. They carried a camera that allowed Apollo 11 to broadcast T.V. pictures of the astronauts stepping down onto the Moon's surface. This is what Neil Armstrong said when he put his foot on the Moon, "That's one small step for a man; one giant leap for mankind."

They took pictures and planted an American flag on the Moon's surface after exploring it for nearly two and a half hours. They collected soil and rocks to bring back to Earth. These samples have helped scientists learn about the Moon's surface and its interior.

Did you know there was another important member of the team who brought them back to Earth? His name was Michael Collins. Apollo 11 spacecraft had two modules. One module carried Neil Armstrong and Buzz Aldrin to the Moon's surface while another called command module with Michael Collins in it, remained in the Moon's orbit. This module brought them back home!

13. What is a spacecraft?

Spacecrafts are huge machines that are used to travel in space. There are different types of spacecraft, each designed in a different way for a different purpose. It is a very risky job to travel in space as we don't have enough information about the climate, pressure, and gravity on other planets and objects in space. So, we don't know how our bodies will react in unknown conditions. Hence, scientists cannot always send an astronaut in space.

Sometimes small, robotic spacecraft are sent to explore planets, moons, comets, and asteroids in our Solar System. These machines are sent without astronauts and are called space probes. There are many types of space probes such as orbiters, landers and rovers.

So, what do we call a spacecraft that takes astronauts into space? It is called a space shuttle. A space shuttle lands on a planet. It does not just carry astronauts but also space probes that can be left in the space while the space shuttle comes back to Earth.

14. What do space probes like flybys, orbiters, landers and rovers do in space?

Space probes travel through space to collect information from different planets, their moons, asteroids and comets. They send this information back to Earth for scientists to study. Space probes transmit data from space by radio waves which scientists on Earth study. These probes carry special cameras and instruments to take photographs and bring rock and soil samples. While some of these probes come back to Earth with data and samples they collect, some only make a one-way journey. Let's look at some of these cool machines and what they do:

Flybys: They collect information while flying past the objects in space.

Landers & Rovers: Landers of course land. But some landers carry rovers that are medium-sized robots. Rovers can move around unlike landers and help to collect data from different angles and places beside the site where they land. They also gather soil and rock samples.

Orbiters: They rotate into an orbit around a planet or moon for some time and gather data for scientists.

All of these amazing machines are controlled from the Earth by very powerful remote controls!

15. Have we explored all the planets in the Solar System?

Yes, we've explored all known planets, except Pluto, in one way or another. Well, we now know that Pluto is not considered a planet anymore! Though we have explored these planets, we have not been able to land on all of these. We have only landed on Venus and Mars while we've observed others either by means of flybys and orbiters. We have also landed on Earth's moon and on Saturn's moon. One spacecraft did manage to enter the atmosphere of Jupiter but the contact was lost before it could be known whether it reached a solid surface or not. However, scientists keep on building the latest spacecraft so that they can continue exploring the space!

16. What do we know about Venus from spacecraft landings?

Venus has proved very unfriendly for spacecraft landings. It is a very hot planet as it is the second planet from the Sun. Though some landers have managed to land on the planet, they were able to send us information for a very short time as the high temperature and pressure of Venus melted and crushed the landers. Scientists have also sent some space shuttles to orbit around Venus which have sent some important information. For example, the surface of Venus has more than 1,000 volcanoes. It is also called Earth's twin as Earth and Venus are very similar in size.

Well, even before scientists explored Venus through satellites and spacecraft, we have long known Venus as the second brightest object in the night sky next only to the Moon. It is because it is the closest object to Earth besides the Moon. It's visible a couple of hours before sunrise and after sunset. Many years ago, people used to think that Venus was two different stars but it was the Greek mathematician Pythagoras who discovered that the brightest stars in the morning and evening sky were, in fact, the same object, Venus. That is why it is also known as the Morning Star and the Evening Star.

17. What do we know about Mars from many scientific explorations?

Mars has long been known as the red planet. It looks reddish-orange from the Earth. Mars is the most explored planets of all. Scientists have sent highly advanced robots who have gathered samples of soil and rocks from Mars's surface. They have managed to get important scientific data from these visits. Let's have a look at some cool information about Mars:

The red colour of Mars is due to the rock and dust covering its surface. These rocks are rich in iron.

Mars is a very cold, dry planet, where liquid water cannot exist on the surface. The average temperature is 63 degrees Celsius below zero, which is very similar to winters in Antarctica.

Mars has both North and South polar ice caps, just like Earth. There is also a lot of ice in the frozen ground, similar to the areas of northern Canada and Russia.

It has mountain ranges, volcanic fields, valleys, ice caps, canyons and deserts.

18. Mars has so many similarities with Earth. Is it possible to find life there?

With so many Mars explorations, we now know that no life form exists on Mars today. It is a really cold planet and lacks a thick atmosphere that helps to trap some heat. But scientists have reasons to believe there was once life on Mars. What is one basic requirement for any organism to grow? It is water.

In a very famous mission, a lander called Pathfinder was sent on Mars. It sent back thousands of photographs that suggested that water once flowed over the surface of Mars. Further missions helped scientists gather more useful data. There were clear pictures of channels that look like dry river beds. These channels, plains and canyons hint at the possibility that they were created by water erosion in the past. There is also evidence of minerals that can only be formed in water. In addition to this, in 1996, a group of scientists found evidence of bacteria inside a meteorite that had come from Mars. All of these evidence point that there was once life on Mars. But we can never be sure!

Space is no longer a mystery now. Many astronauts have explored the space and know what the stars and planets are made of and how big they are. Now, this is really some cool stuff!

19. What does it take to become an astronaut?

Almost all the earlier astronauts were pilots. They knew how to deal with speed, danger and challenge. Neil Armstrong, the first man to walk on the moon, was a test pilot before he became an astronaut. Yuri Gagarin, the first man to go into space, was a jet fighter pilot. Today, astronauts need to have a lot of knowledge about computer technology. All the controls of the spacecraft are now controlled through computers.

All astronauts go through intensive training. Space missions are very dangerous and can be very expensive. Astronauts need to be trained on how to deal with emergencies. For example, the craft may run out of fuel, then the craft needs to be brought back for an immediate landing. They also need to learn to deal with weightlessness in space as there is no gravity there.

20. What do astronauts eat in space?

If an astronaut drops his burger, it will float in the air. And if his water spills, the water will not fall into the cup. It will float in the air! If water floats in the air, you know it can damage the spacecraft. So how do they manage to eat in space where there is no gravity?

Astronauts need a good dose of vitamins to stay active and alert while living in space. Earlier, astronauts ate food packed in the form of a toothpaste. They squeezed food like apple sauce into their mouths. Then later the new method was to dry the food, suck out the water and then pack. But this was not the kind of food astronauts would enjoy eating. A lot of effort was made to design ways to serve better food in space. In 1970, a special warm tray was invented to keep the food warm and a fridge to keep vegetables and fruits fresh. Special cups with inbuilt straws were made so that astronauts could drink water and cold drinks. Since then the astronauts are enjoying tasty and healthy food!

21. Is Lance Armstrong brother of Neil Armstrong?

No, they are not brothers but they both are surely famous.

Lance Armstrong is a road racing cyclist from America. He won Tour De France (road race cycling championship) 7 times consecutively! But he was disqualified in 2012 because of charges of doping (using drugs to enhance performance in sports which is illegal). He is the founder of Livestrong Foundation, an organisation that provides support to cancer patients. In 1996, he was diagnosed with cancer which he fought bravely.

22. Has any animal also gone into space?

Scientists have tried to send flies, beetles, wasps and monkeys into space since 1947. They wanted to test first with animals if living beings can survive in space. They first sent a fruit fly and then a monkey to find out if they could survive. In November 1957, the Russians sent a dog named Laika into space. She was the first animal to orbit the Earth. She travelled in a spacecraft named Sputnik2.

23. How does Earth's atmosphere make it a better place to live?

The earth is surrounded by a blanket of air called atmosphere. This blanket of air is made up of many layers of gases. One of the most important gases in the Earth's atmosphere is Oxygen. We need Oxygen to breathe. Another gas which plays a very important role is Ozone. It forms a layer in the atmosphere known as the Ozone layer. Ozone layer blocks some of the harmful UV rays of the Sun.

But did you know some manmade activities are harming the Ozone layer? We use gases such as CFCs (Chloro-Fluoro-Carbons) to make soaps, foams, pesticides, fire extinguishers, refrigerators and air conditioners. These gases reach the atmosphere and destroy the Ozone layer. Hence, the Ozone layer is getting thinner.

24. Why don't dinosaurs live anymore?

Dinosaurs used to live on the Earth but then 65 million years ago, they went extinct. Yes, this sounds like an awfully long time, isn't it! When we say extinct, it means they stopped living. Nobody knows for sure why dinosaurs went extinct but scientists have some interesting guesses to what might have happened so many years ago.

Meteor: Some scientists believe that a meteor might have crashed into Earth, causing lots of dust and heat. The dust may have blocked the sunlight for so long that many plants and animals, including dinosaurs, did not survive.

Volcanic Eruption: There are some scientists who think that a huge volcanic eruption or a big earthquake created some changes in the environment at the time dinosaurs lived. The dinosaurs could not live in the new environment and died.

25. What did dinosaurs look like?

Dinosaur is a Greek word that means a 'fearfully great lizard'. Dinosaurs looked like huge lizards. From sluggish, plant-eating giants to violent hunters, there were all kinds of dinosaurs that dominated the Earth for over 160 million years. They lived on land, swam in the water and there were flying dinosaurs too. They had all sorts of interesting features that might have helped them survive the conditions of the times they lived in. They had horns, plates, thorns, spines, long necks, and claws. Some of the widely-known dinosaurs are:

Stegosaurus: It was a slow-moving plant-eater that had spikes on its tail. It had a small head with a brain the size of an orange.

Tyrannosaurus: Also known as T-Rex, it was a fierce meat-eating dinosaur. Its powerful jaw had 60 teeth and scientists have found its teeth mark on the fossil bones of other dinosaurs. These marks suggest that T-Rex could crunch through the bones!

Diplodocus: It had a very long neck to reach high vegetation. It was one of the largest animals that have ever lived on Earth! Did you know how much it weighed? Close to 50 tons!

Triceratops: It had 3 horns, a parrot-like beak, and a large frill. This plant-eater had a massive skull that could reach nearly 1 metre.

26. If dinosaurs got extinct so many years ago, how do we know that they even existed?

Scientists have found body parts or remains of dinosaurs buried under the Earth. They have dug up parts such as bones, teeth, claws, etc from many places around the world. Sometimes they are able to dig a complete dinosaur body. These remains are called Fossils. Scientists have an amazing ability to study these fossils, do chemical tests on them and come up with new information. This information tells us what they ate and how they might have looked like. Though all this information may not always be correct as we don't have real dinosaurs to compare, but we get to know quite a bit about dinosaurs from these fossils.

27. But not all dinosaurs got extinct. Some lived on. Do you know birds are living dinosaurs?

Yes, that is true. Scientists have discovered that birds evolved from dinosaurs. They have found many fossils of ancient animals with both bird and dinosaur features. For example, they found a fossil called Archaeopteryx had lived 147 million years ago. Archaeopteryx had a feathered tail and wings just like modern birds. But it also had dinosaur features such as a bony tail and 3 fingers ending in claws.

Scientists believe that as the environment of Earth changed, not all dinosaurs died. Some dinosaurs were able to survive. Nature changed their shapes and size so that they could adjust to the new surroundings and they turned into birds. This process is called evolution.

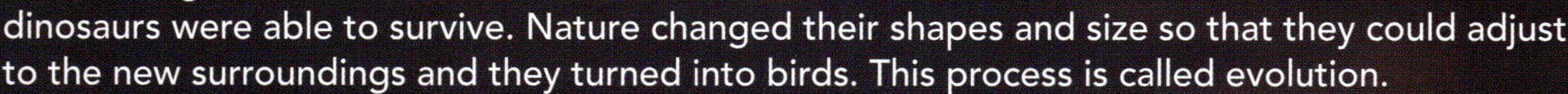

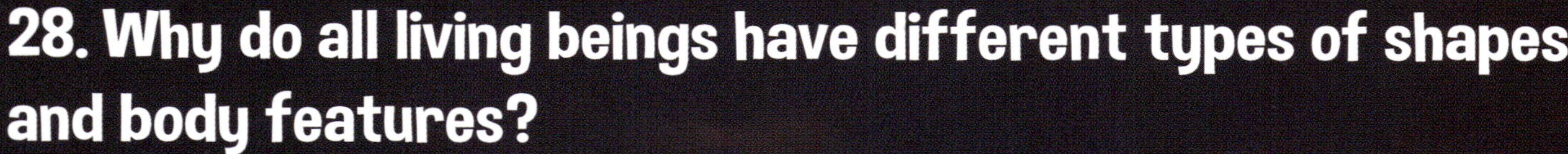

28. Why do all living beings have different types of shapes and body features?

Have you noticed how different human beings, birds and animals are from each other? In fact all animals are not alike either. There are so many types or species of animals and birds. Some animals live in water while some live on land. Some live near icebergs while others live on trees. Every animal has its own special and unique features, traits and behaviour. These unique features help them to adapt and survive in their special living conditions. For example, the animals that live in water have gills to breathe while those on land breathe with lungs. Let's have a look at some other interesting examples:

Cactus plants don't have leaves but spikes to help them survive in the desert where there is very little water!

Camels have special humps to store food and water to survive in the hot desert!

Owls have special eyes to help them see better in the dark! Can you see in the dark that clearly? No way. It's because we don't need to stay awake at night to get our food like owls do.

29. You must have heard the word 'species' many times but do you know what it actually means?

Scientists have categorised living beings according to the same type of features, traits and behaviour that they show. Let's take an example. If you visit a library, how do you find your favourite book? It is usually in the children's section. There are sections for grownups and teens too. All these sections are further divided into other categories such as fiction, biographies, science, mystery, etc. The librarian has neatly categorised the books according to their types.

In the same way, scientists have categorised living beings. So, a group of living beings that have the same type of features and characteristics is called species. Sometimes, we can see these features while some may not be visible to us as they are inside the body. Scientists often decide whether two groups of animals or plants are the same species by figuring out whether or not they can mate with each other. If we try and get a rose to make seeds with cauliflower it won't work as they are separate species. But if you try and get a rose to make seeds with another rose, it will work as they belong to the same species.

30. Did you know million and millions of years ago humans looked like apes too?

Yes, we had tails, sharp teeth, dark skin and lots of body hair. But over a period of time, we evolved. We developed some unique features and lost the ones that we didn't need. For example:

- We started walking on two legs so we were now able to use tools and work with our hands.
- We invented fire and started cooking our food rather than eating it raw. This made our teeth less sharper.
- We started wearing clothes to keep warm or even to protect ourselves from the harmful rays of the Sun as our body hair

started getting shorter and thinner.

This process of evolution helped humans to be different than the rest of the animals.

31. But why is there a need to evolve?

Let's try to understand it like this: If you live in a hot climate and plan a vacation to a place that is extremely cold, what would you do? You will wear warm clothes and eat food that gives you more energy to stay warm. You are trying to adapt to a new environment to stay healthy and alive. Being able to evolve, adapt and change to meet new situations makes it possible for living things to survive! The ones who are not able to survive the change, die. This is called the survival of the fittest. So in a way, nature selects the best. This theory of natural selection was first observed by a great scientist who studied nature very closely. His name was Charles Darwin.

32. Who was Charles Darwin?

Charles Darwin was the great scientist who loved studying nature. He lived much of his life in England but he took a famous five-year voyage on a ship called the HMS Beagle. The ship sailed through South America and the southern oceans. What did he do there?

He found different fossils in these places and related them to modern animals. He realised that same species have evolved into something different in new surroundings.

He observed how different animals compete with each other for food. He also noticed that the strongest animals were most likely to survive and pass their traits down to their children. This leads to the formation of new species which keeps on evolving into further new species.

He published all his observations in a book and introduced the theory of evolution for the first time.

33. Did you know all living things have evolved over billions of years from a single common ancestor?

It might seem strange to think that you and your pet may have a common ancestor many, many years ago. Scientists believe that all life on Earth evolved from a single-celled organism that lived around 3.5 billion years ago. So, did you also share your ancestor with the frog that just hopped by?

Well, Charles Darwin seemed to think so. He believed that if we keep tracing back our family tree, other species would also join in. Ultimately, all living beings will be traced to one common ancestor. Pretty cool, isn't it? He suggested that new species keep on evolving with the changes in their environment. And that is what may have happened so many years ago. Though we all started as the same species, we all evolved into different species according to our needs.

34. Why do we get fever?

What will you do if a stranger enters your house without permission and tries to harm you? You will fight him to save yourself of course. And what will you need to fight? A stick sounds a good idea! So, when some germs (virus or bacteria) enter our body, our body doesn't like it at all. It fights back and tries to throw them out. And what do you think the body fights the germs with? Let's find out:

When germs enter our body, it produces white blood cells and antibodies. White blood cells and antibodies fight and kill germs. They release chemicals that raise the body temperature. The increase in body temperature produces heat in the body. This kills the germs because germs cannot tolerate heat. So when you have a fever it is a sign that our body is fighting and killing the germs. Though it's a sign that your body is working against infection, you should always visit a doctor when you have a fever.

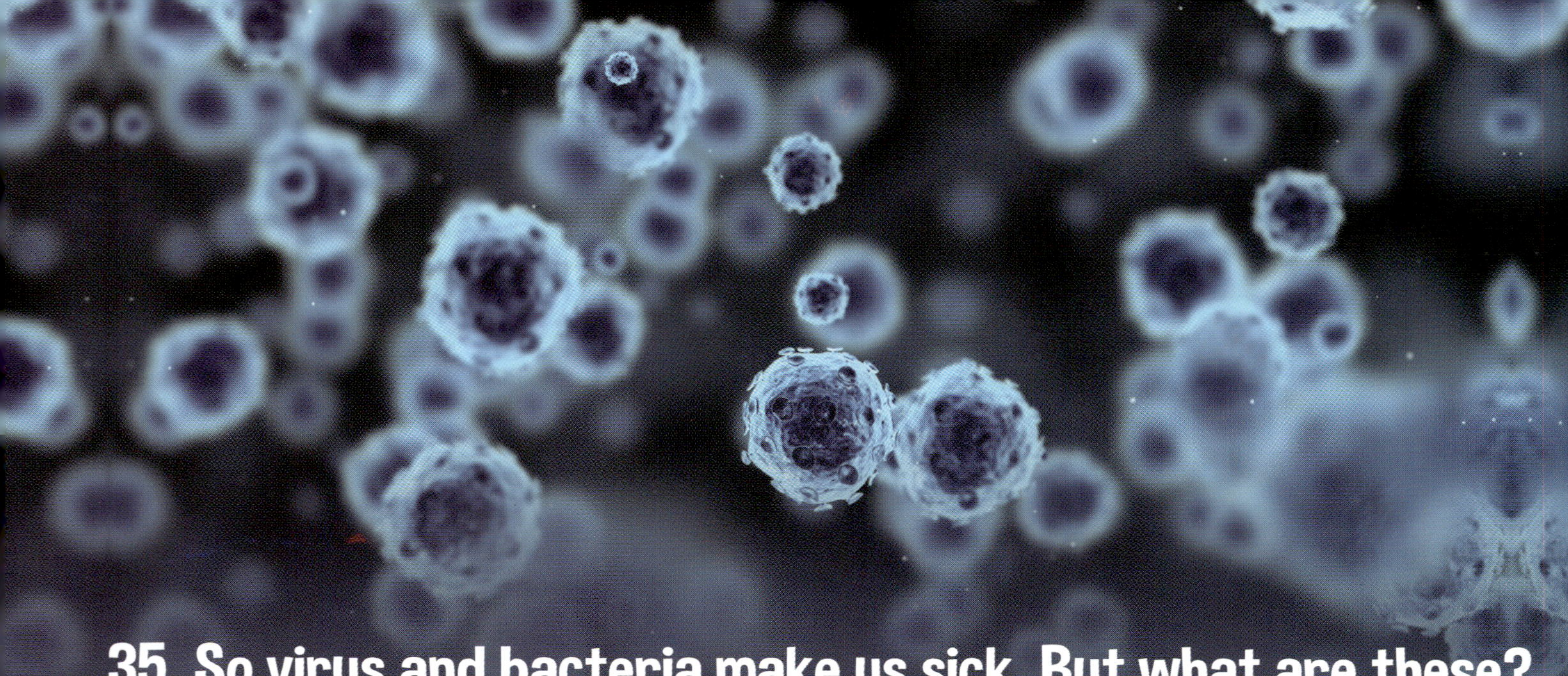

35. So virus and bacteria make us sick. But what are these?

If you are put in a room alone and then asked to point out to another living thing, what will be your reaction? You would say there is no living thing here other than me, right? But there are very small living things all around you. These tiny creatures are called microorganisms. (Micro means small and organism means living being). Viruses and bacteria are types of microorganisms. Some can make us really sick while some are actually good for the body and nature. They are so small that we cannot see them with our eyes. We need special instruments like a microscope to spot them.

36. What is a virus?

A virus is a small bundle of chemicals. It is present all around us, in the air or on your table, chair and even on your toys. It cannot survive on its own for long. It can only grow when it enters the cells of other living beings. All living beings and even non-living beings are made from cells. A virus can enter the body through our eyes, nose, mouth or even break into our skin. Once it enters the body, it grows in numbers, attacks our cells and infects them. This can make us really sick.

But our body tries to fight the infection back by making white blood cells. White blood cells make antibodies to fight and kill the virus. We might need medicines too when we get infected from a virus but medicines can't kill a virus completely. It can only stop them from growing fast.

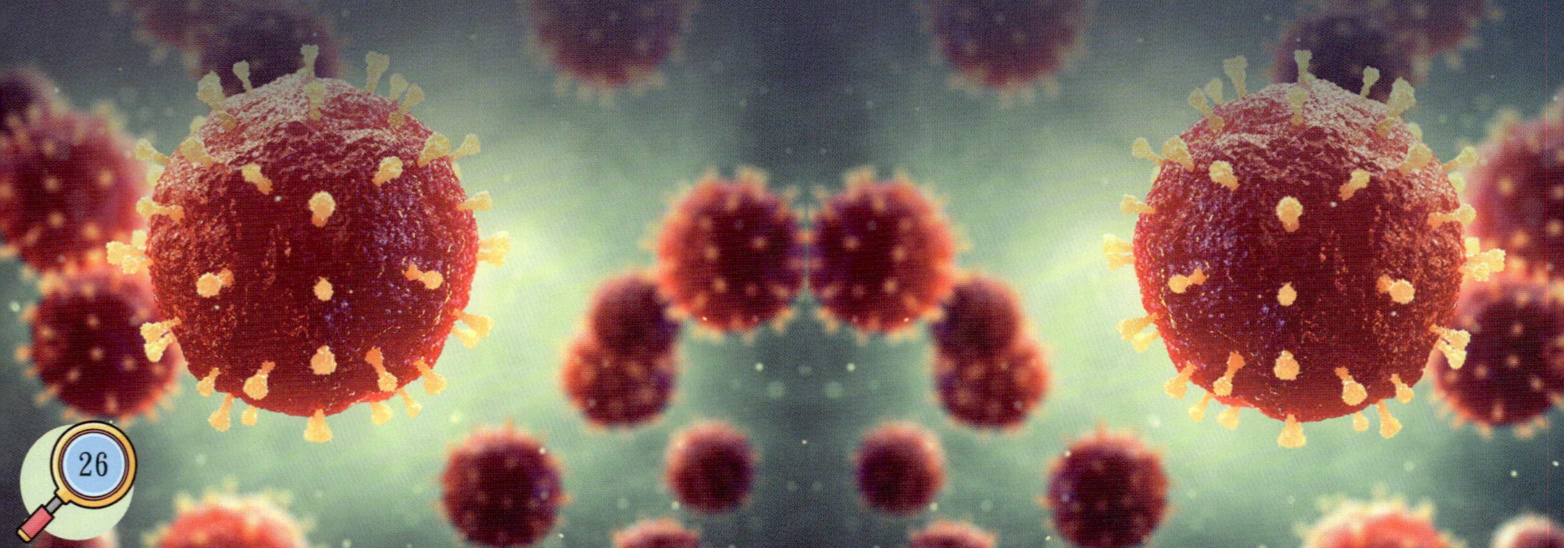

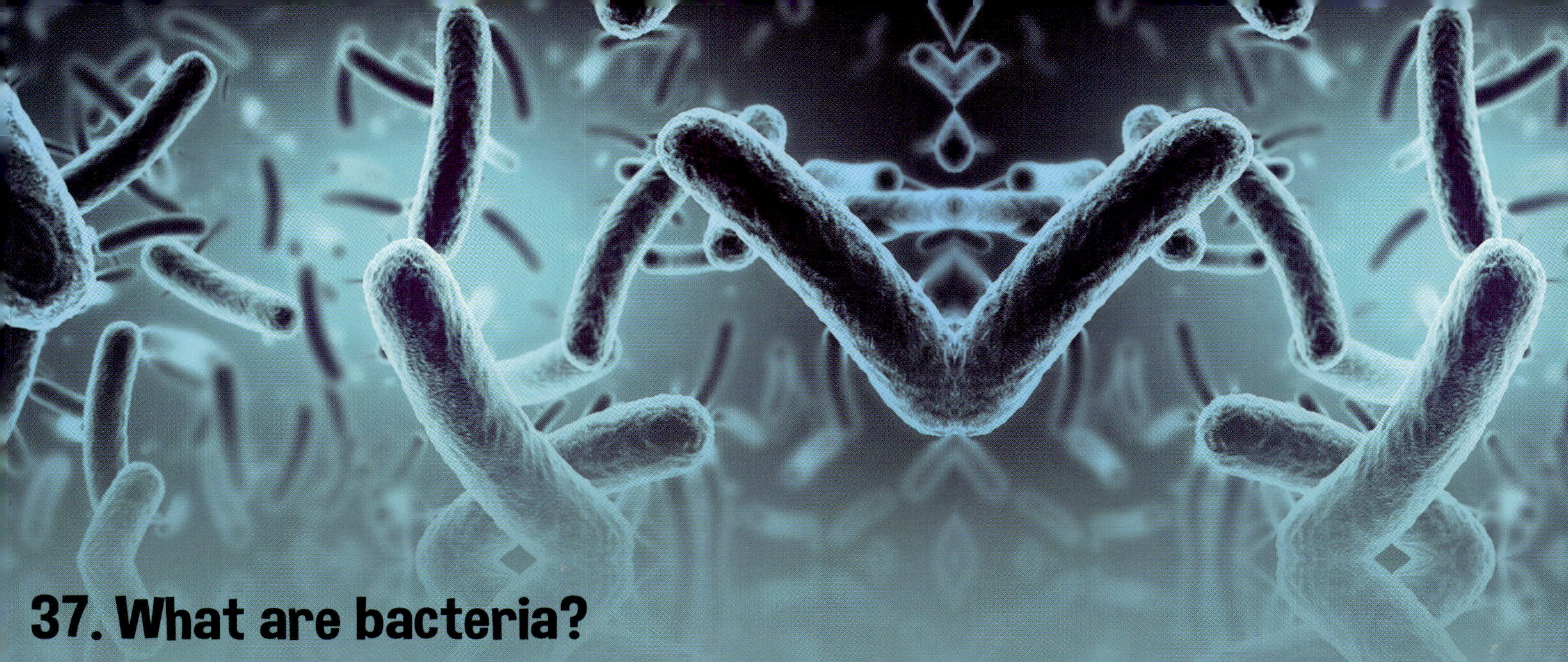

37. What are bacteria?

Bacteria are tiny living beings that are present everywhere, even inside our bodies. But they are different from virus. They don't need a living cell to grow and can pretty much grow anywhere. But just like virus, they can make us sick. The good news is that medicines can kill bacteria and help us get well soon. But not all bacteria are bad; some even help us to stay healthy. Isn't that strange? But it is absolutely true.

38. What are the good bacteria and how do they help us?

Some bacteria are really good helpers. They help us in so many ways:

Digest food: These bacteria are present in saliva, stomach and intestines and break food into smaller particles.

Curd: Some special bacteria help the milk to turn into curd. Curd makes the intestines healthy and helps to digest food. It is full of calcium and also helps us to build immunity.

Medicines: If you have viral or flu, the doctor gives you antibiotics. These are made with the help of microorganisms. They are also used to make vaccines that prevent diseases like polio, small pox, typhoid etc.

Decomposition: All the waste needs to be broken down into smaller matter. This process is called decomposition. Microorganisms help in decomposition. This decomposed waste is used in soil to make it fertile so that we can grow vegetables and flowers!

39. Do you remember your parents taking you for vaccination when you were young? Do you know what vaccination is?

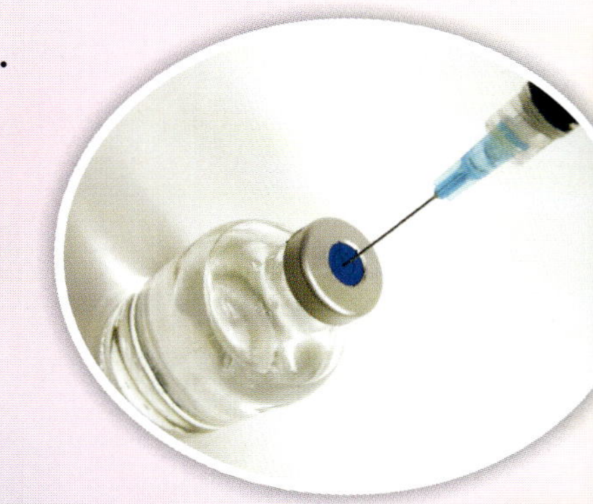

Our body can catch all kinds of diseases caused by virus or bacteria. Vaccination protects our body from some of these diseases. A vaccine is nothing but the same virus or bacteria but in a very small quantity. For example, to prevent measles, the doctor will inject you with a very small dose of the weakened virus of measles.

Sounds strange? But why would we inject a virus in the body that can cause us a disease? Here, let us take the example of measles. When we inject this weakened virus of measles, the body will react to it. It will create antibodies to fight measles. What is so amazing with our body is that once it makes an antibody to fight a specific disease, it always stays in the body. So the next time measles attacks you, your antibodies will fight it and you will not even know this. The body will thus 'remember' the infection and learn to fight it without making us sick every time. This is called building the immunity of the body.

40. What is immunity?

Grownups say that you have a weak immunity when we get sick too often. Or that you have a strong immunity when you don't catch cold or fever often. Immunity is the ability of our body to fight the germs and infections. Our body has our immune system that fights with germs and infections and keeps the body strong. White blood cells are part of this immune system. Healthy food, good sleep and exercise makes our immunity strong. Do you now know why your mom asks you to eat healthy all the time? Yes, it's because it will make you less sick.

41. Food rich in vitamins and minerals is healthy. What do vitamins and minerals do?

Our body needs nutrition to stay healthy and get energy. So, where does this nutrition comes from? It comes from healthy food that is full of vitamins and minerals. They help us to stay strong, develop strong immune system and carry out different functions properly. While some vitamins help us to see clearly, some vitamins and minerals make your teeth and bones strong.

42. Why are carrots good for you?

Carrots contain Vitamin A. Vitamin A is very good for our eyes. What would happen if you don't get enough vitamin A? You would not be able to see clearly in dim lights as it affects your vision. This condition is called night blindness. Deficiency of vitamin A also decreases the immunity of our body.

Can you name two more food-items that have Vitamin A in them? —Pumpkins and spinach.

43. Why should you have oranges?

Oranges contain Vitamin C. Vitamin C helps our body in so many ways. It helps the body to fight cold. It also helps the body to heal itself if you get a cut. Not only that, it helps the body to absorb a very important mineral called iron.

Food items rich in Vitamin C are usually sour. Lemon and Grapefruit are rich in Vitamin C.

44. Why is milk good for you?

Milk has the mineral Calcium. Calcium makes your bones and teeth very strong. All things made from milk have calcium in it. Can you name some foods that are made from milk? Cheese, curd and custard! But our body needs Vitamin D along with calcium. Vitamin D helps the body to absorb the calcium from the food we eat. Where do we get Vitamin D from? Sunlight is the main source of Vitamin D. It is also found in some foods such as fish and egg yolks.

45. Why is apple good for you?

Apple has iron. Iron is a mineral that helps the body to make healthy red blood cells. What would happen if your body doesn't get enough iron? You will get a disease called anaemia. It makes you very weak and inactive. Iron is also found in spinach and egg yolk.

46. Did you know that some of the foods we eat resemble the body part they help become strong?

That sounds pretty interesting.

A sliced carrot resembles the pupil and iris in our eyes. We all know that carrot helps to protect and improve the eyesight.

Walnut resembles brain. Walnut helps in the better functioning of nerves which carry information to the brain.

A sliced tomato has four chambers that resemble the structure of a heart. Eating tomatoes reduces the risk of heart diseases.

Kidney beans are shaped like kidneys. They help to heal and maintain kidney functions.

Ginger looks like stomach. It is no wonder than that it helps in digesting the food. It also has the ability to prevent nausea and vomiting.

Celery stalks just look like bones. Celery strengthens the bones.

47. Eyelashes protect our eyes and help us to blink. Why do we need to blink?

Every time we blink, our eyelids spread some moisture across the eyes. This moisture is basically made up of oil and mucus which keeps our eyes wet and moist. This helps us to see clearly all the time. Blinking also helps to protect the eyes from dust and bright lights around us.

48. How do our nasal hair (hair in the nose) protect us?

When we breathe, we also inhale some particles present in the air around us such as dust, dirt, germs and pollen. These unwanted particles can reach our lungs and infect them, making it tough to breathe. The tiny bush of hair in our nose stops these particles. Therefore, the nasal hair create a shield between our lungs and the unwanted particles in the air that can harm us.

49. The mucous in our nose makes us all stuffy but did you know it's very important?

There is some sticky, slimy stuff that keeps our nose wet and moist. It is called mucous. It also helps our nasal hair to trap the particles that can harm our body if we breathe them. When the mucus, dirt and other trapped particles get dry in the nose, we are left with a booger.

When you have a cold or flu, our nose makes more mucous to keep germs out of our lungs. This extra mucous runs down our throat or out of our nose! Sometimes it just sits there making us all stuffy.

50. Your hair makes you look good. But did you know it has other important functions too?

It helps us like a helmet: It acts as a cushion and protects the head from minor bumps.

It helps you like fur: It acts as a cap in winters and gives you warmth.

It helps you like a hat: It acts as a shield in summers. It prevents the burning sun rays to fall directly on your scalp.

51. Achoo! Achoo! Achoo! Is common cold the only reason that makes us sneeze so much?

There can be so many reasons that can make us go Aaaachoo!

When something enters your nose, it sends a signal to your brain that some foreign particle has entered your nose. It makes you sneeze so that your nose can throw this out. It helps to keep your nose clean and stop the bacteria, viruses and dust to enter inside your body.

You also sneeze when you have a cold or a viral infection. As tiny as they are, viruses can cause nasal swelling and irritation that can trigger sneezing.

Have you ever noticed that paints have this strange, sharp smell? This sharp smell is due to chemicals that are used to make the paint. When you smell these chemicals, you sneeze.

Allergy makes you sneeze too.

52. What is an allergy?

Usually, when something harmful comes in contact with your body, it reacts. This reaction may cause sneezing, watery eyes, skin rashes, itching and wheezing. We call this allergy. But some people develop allergies from things that are otherwise not harmful to others. For example, nuts, mushrooms, fish, strawberries, eggs, milk, etc. These are healthy foods but some people get allergy from them. It is strange but true. So, if you eat, touch or smell something and get symptoms like this, it means you are allergic to that particular thing.

It's a little complicated to talk about allergies. Doctors and scientists are still doing lots of research on why we get allergies. Some people have a very sensitive immune system and that's why they react like this.

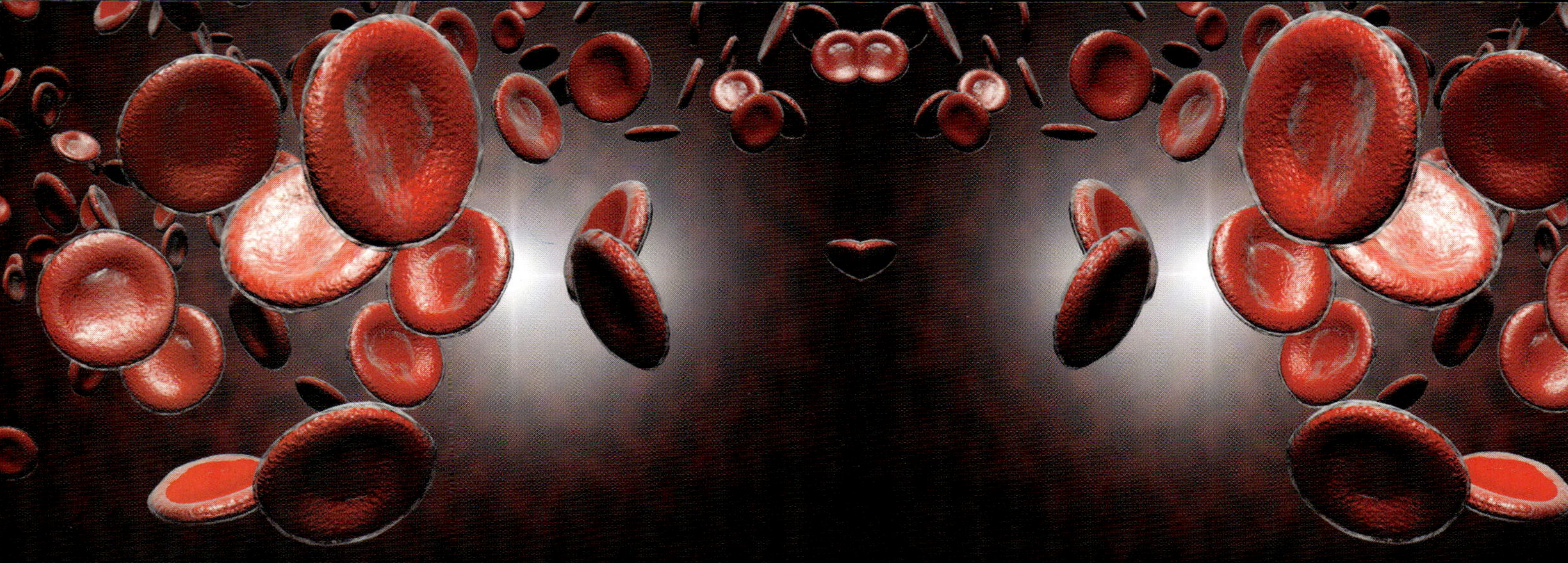

53. What is blood made up of?

Remember the times when you got some minor cuts on fingers or had scraped your knees. You must have seen blood oozing out from these cuts. It happens when you injure the blood vessels under your skin and blood flows out. So, what is this red liquid made up of? Blood is made up of red blood cells, white blood cells and platelets floating in a yellow liquid called plasma. Are you wondering where do all these cells and plasma come from?

Plasma is made by the body from what we eat and drink. It is made up of proteins, glucose, nutrients, chemicals and hormones. More than half of the blood is plasma. It carries nutrition for the body.

Red blood cells, white blood cells, and platelets are made by our bones.

54. More than half of the blood is plasma. If plasma is yellow in colour, why is blood red?

Blood contains red blood cells. These cells are made up of a protein called haemoglobin. Haemoglobin contains iron, which gives red colour to our blood. Do you know what red blood cells do? They carry oxygen around our body and give energy to all the organs in the body. Our organs need oxygen to function properly.

55. What do white blood cells do?

White blood cells are like little warriors floating in your blood. They fight germs like viruses and bacteria. Usually, when we stay healthy, the amount of white blood cells is less in our blood. It is only when we get sick that our body makes more of white blood cells to fight the germs attacking us.

56. When we have a minor cut or an injury, we bleed a little. Have you noticed how bleeding stops on its own? Why is that so?

Blood stops flowing on its own after a minor cut as there are some sticky cells present in the blood. These sticky cells are called platelets. When there is a cut, these platelets join or clump together to make the blood thick at the site of the injury. As a result, a very soft lump called a clot is formed that plugs the cut and it stops bleeding after a while. When we lose small amounts of blood, our body makes new blood cells and quickly replaces the lost blood. But sometimes in big accidents, people lose large amounts of blood that can't be replaced by the body so fast. In these cases, doctors can use blood from one person and give it to another. It is called a blood transfusion.

57. Sometimes when we are very sick, the doctor asks us to get some blood tests done. Why do we need to do this?

Doctors suggest a blood test to see what is making you feel sick or tired. A nurse will use a syringe or a very thin needle to draw a few drops of blood from under your skin. What do you think they are taking the blood out from? Yes, a blood vessel of course. It doesn't hurt more than a mosquito bite! This sample of blood is put into a bottle and labelled with your name. It then goes to a lab and is looked at under a microscope.

So what do the doctors look for? Your blood can actually provide a lot of information. The doctor would want to look at the number of red blood cells, white blood cells and platelets to see what can be wrong with you! He also checks for the levels of chemicals, proteins, glucose and hormones that are present in the blood. All these things should be present within a range. If their amount is more than or less than this range, it means there is a problem and our body is not functioning properly. The doctor identifies the problem and gives us medicines accordingly.

58. We can all feel the thumping lub-dub sound of our heart behind our chest. It is called a heart beat. But do you have any idea what is really going on in there? What makes our heart beat?

Clasp both of your hands together. This is how big your heart is! Our heart is, in fact, a very powerful muscle. It has a very special function too. It circulates fresh blood in our bodies. It is like a pump that has two sides; a right-side and a left-side.

The right side of our heart receives blood from the body and pumps it to the lungs.

The left side of the heart receives blood from the lungs and pumps it back to the body.

Both the right and the left sides have two valves each. These valves open and close to let the blood come in and go out of the heart. As these valves open and close, the valves make the sound we hear as our heartbeat!

59. How do heart and lungs work together to pump pure blood to the body?

We know that blood carries oxygen and nutrition to the body organs. When the blood has delivered its oxygen to the body parts, it goes back to the heart to get an oxygen refill.

This oxygen-less blood also contains some waste material such as carbon dioxide.

The right side of the heart receives this impure blood and sends it to the lungs.

In the lungs, the blood picks up more oxygen and gives up carbon dioxide.

The blood is now full of oxygen and enters the heart through the left side. The heart then pumps this fresh blood back to the body organs.

Where does so much oxygen in the lungs come from? The air that we breathe in provides oxygen to the lungs. And what happens to the carbon dioxide in the lungs? We exhale the carbon dioxide out of the lungs.

60. How does the blood travel through our body?

There are long tubes inside our bodies that carry blood within them. These tubes are also called blood vessels. There is a huge network of blood vessels in our bodies. If we laid all our blood vessels down, from end to end, they will be about 60,000 miles long for a child and about 100,000 miles for an adult!

The blood vessels carrying fresh blood from the heart to the body are called Arteries. (Also called red blood vessels.)

The blood vessels carrying the impure blood from the body to the heart are called Veins. (Also called blue blood vessels.)

61. During Halloween, we see all the zombies, ghosts and skeletons walking around and it is fun for sure! Are skeletons for real?

We all have a skeleton. Inside our skin, we have one big skeleton. It is made up of big and small bones joined together. So what does this skeleton do? Okay. Remember how you make a tent house to play in. First, you use plastic rods to make a structure. Then, you cover it with a sheet. This is what bones do in our body. They give us a structure and we call it a skeleton. Imagine how would you look if you had no bones in our body? You would jiggle and wiggle like jelly or may be just droop like a ragdoll. Bones helps us to bend, walk, stand and run.

Can you feel some bones in front of your chest? These are bones that shield important organs such as heart and lungs from minor injuries. This set of bones is called a rib-cage. So, bones also help us to protect many important organs in the body.

62. Are bones hollow or solid?

No, all the bones are not solid. Inside the bones, there is gooey stuff called bone marrow. Bone marrow makes red blood cells, white blood cells and platelets. These cells go in our blood and help our bodies to be strong and healthy. Do you remember what these blood cells do? White blood cells help us to fight infections. Red blood cells carry oxygen around the body and platelets help us to stop bleeding after an injury.

63. How many bones are there in a human body?

There are 206 bones in the human body. In fact, a baby is born with 300 bones but as it grows, some bones fuse together and the number gets down to 206. If bones are so hard and strong, how do they not make us stiff? How are we able to bend these hard bones? Well, we don't have long bones continuously. They are joined with one another at places known as joints. These joints make it possible for us to bend our knees, back and elbows.

Thigh bone (Femur) is the strongest and longest bone in the body. It joins your hip to the knee. In fact, all the bones in your legs are quite strong. Do you know why? When you stand up or walk, your legs carry all your body weight. So, they better be strong.

The ear has the smallest and the lightest bone in the body and it is present in the inside of the ear. It is called stapes.

64. How can a doctor tell us if we have a broken bone? He cannot look through the skin after all!

If you have bumped yourself really hard, it is possible that your doctor might want to find out if you have any broken bones. The doctor will usually ask you to get an X-ray test done to find this out. X-ray machines seem to do the impossible. They can see straight through our clothes, skin and even through metal. During the test, an X-ray machine sends some rays through the body, and an image of the internal body organs is recorded on a special film or a computer. Doctors can read this image and tell us if there is a problem. Does it hurt to get an X-ray test done? Not at all! X-rays are totally painless. You can't see or feel them!

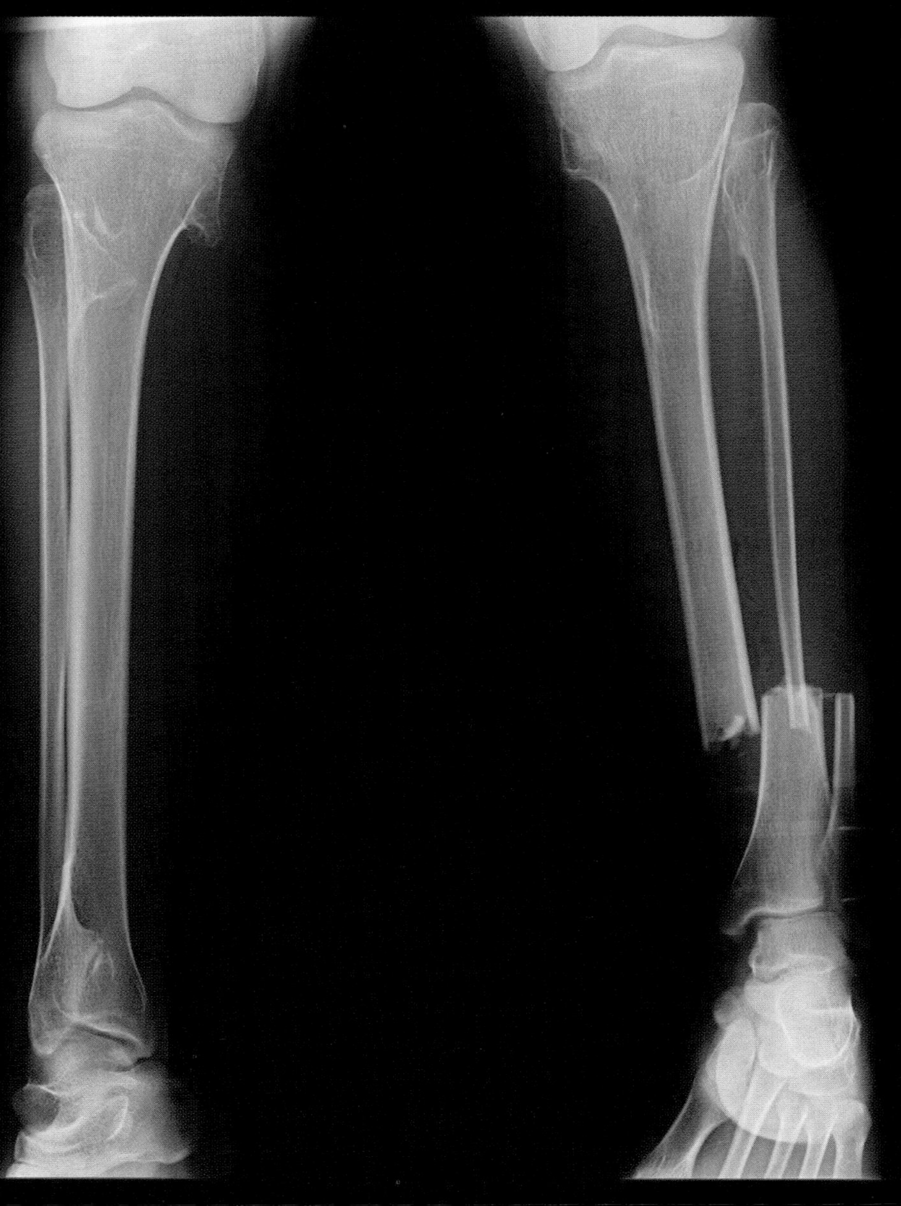

65. Which is the biggest organ in your body?

Are you ready to get surprised? It is the skin. Yes, the skin is actually one of the organs. It covers everything that is inside of our body. Without our skin, all the bones, muscles and organs would be hanging out. The skin holds everything in place. It protects our body and keeps it at the right temperature. It helps us to stay warm in winter and stay cool in summers. It also makes Vitamin D which is very important to keep your bones healthy and strong. Can you think of something else that you can do with your skin? Yes, it helps us feel things by touch. We can feel if something is hot, cold, soft or hard. The skin is not only the largest organ; it is also the largest sensory organ of our body.

66. What is a sensory organ?

A sensory organ helps us to explore the world around us. It gives us information on things that surround us and lets us know how to react and respond to these. We have five sensory organs in our body that give us five senses:

Our skin helps us to feel things we touch.

Our ears help us to hear.

Our eyes help us to see.

Our nose helps us to smell.

Our tongue helps us to taste.

These senses help us to understand and enjoy the world we live in. They also protect us from harmful things around us by giving us signals and making us alert. So, how does it all work? The sensory organs contain special messengers called nerves. The nerves carry messages from the body to the brain and tell us what is going on around us.

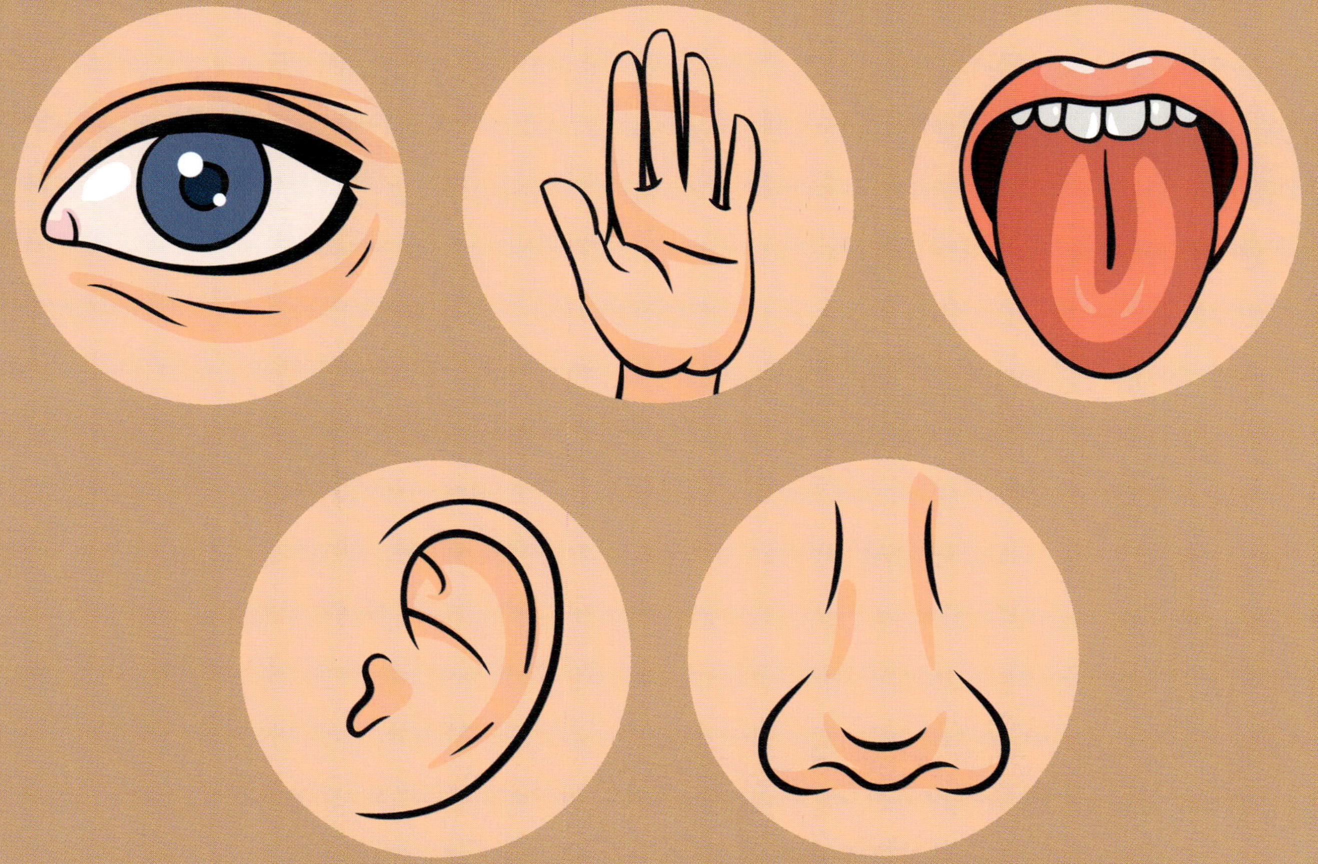

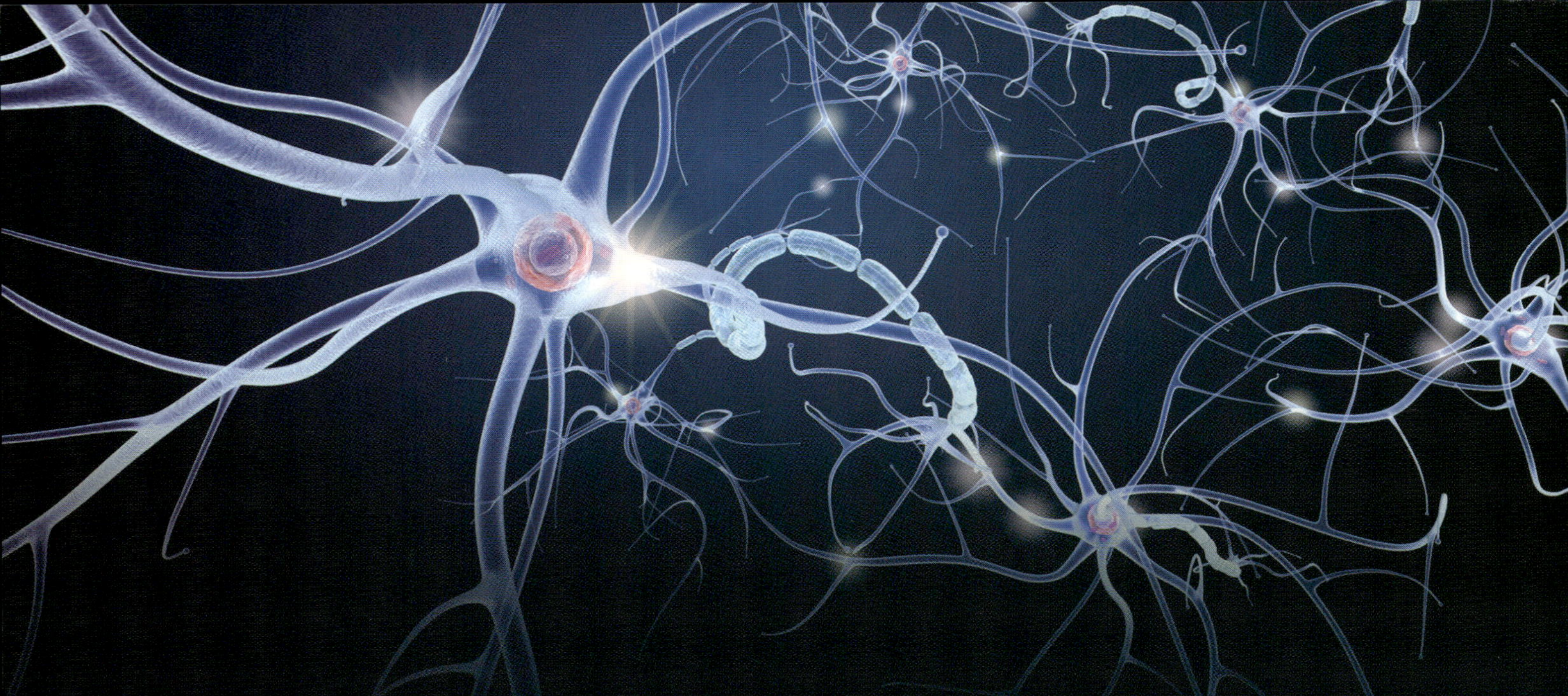

67. What are nerves?

Nerves are thread-like structures that run throughout our body. They branch out of our spinal cord (backbone) and also from the brain. From there, nerves reach out to every organ in our body. They act as messengers and carry messages back and forth between the brain and different parts of the body. They carry all the information from our surroundings to the brain in special codes. Our brain understands these codes and sends the signals back to the body parts through nerves. Our body responds to the new information with action. So, basically, nerves control each and every action of our body.

68. How does skin sends signals to the brain?

When we touch something, the nerves in the skin send this information to our brain. The brain uses this information to signal back if something we have touched is hot, cold, rough, smooth or prickly. They also make us feel pain if something hurts our skin.

69. Are you wondering how fast these signals travel back and forth?

Nerve signals travel really very fast. How else are we able to respond so quickly to changes around us? Our brain and the nerves work together faster than the fastest internet connection. Think how fast you cover your eyes when you suddenly step out on a bright, sunny day, or how fast you move your hand away if you accidentally touch something super hot like a hot pan. What do you think will happen if the signals didn't travel so fast?

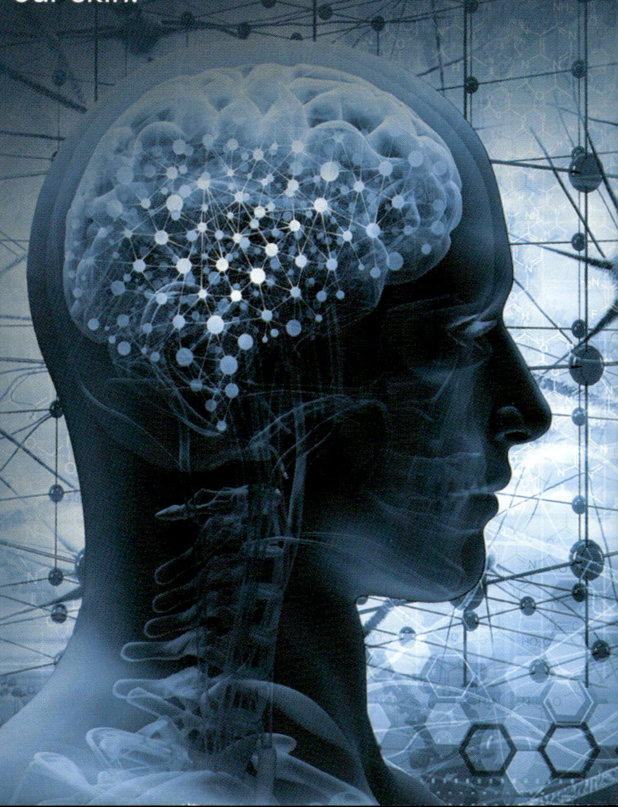

70. Do you like listening to music? Have you ever wondered how you are you able to hear sounds around you?

When a sound wave reaches our ears, it hits the eardrum. The eardrum is a thin layer of skin inside the ear. The sound waves make the eardrum vibrate and with this, the bones behind the eardrum vibrate too. The nerves inside the ears convert these vibrations into signals that the brain can understand. The brain signals back and we understand what the sound is. Remember that your eardrum is very sensitive and fragile. It's never a good idea to put anything in your ear. Even something that seems safe and soft can damage your eardrum. Sometimes, even loud noise can also damage it.

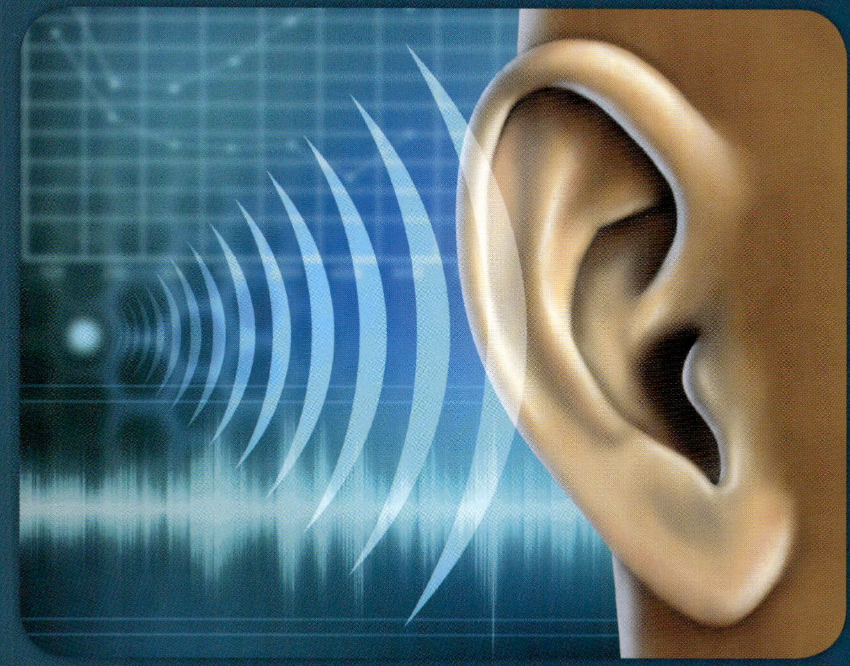

71. Eyes: More than any of the senses, it is the eyes that help us navigate the world around us the most.

In a fraction of seconds, our eyes work with the brain to tell us what we are looking at and what size, colour, texture, and shape it has. Do you know that the eyes work just like a camera? They take pictures of the world around you and send these to the brain. The brain figures out what you are seeing. Let's see what the eyes are made up of.

Pupil: When we look at an object, the light from the object enters our eye through the round black hole called the pupil.

Iris: Pupil is surrounded by a coloured ring-shaped membrane called iris. Iris controls the amount of light that can enter the eye. Too much of light can hurt our eyes!

Lens: The lens of the eyes sits just behind the iris. It focuses the entering light onto the retina to form sharp, clear image of the object.

Retina: It is situated at the back of the eyeball. It is made up of many light receptors called rods and cones.

So this is how we see. When the light from the lens falls onto the retina, the nerves inside the retina turns this light into special signals and carry these to the brain. The brain then tells us what image we are looking at.

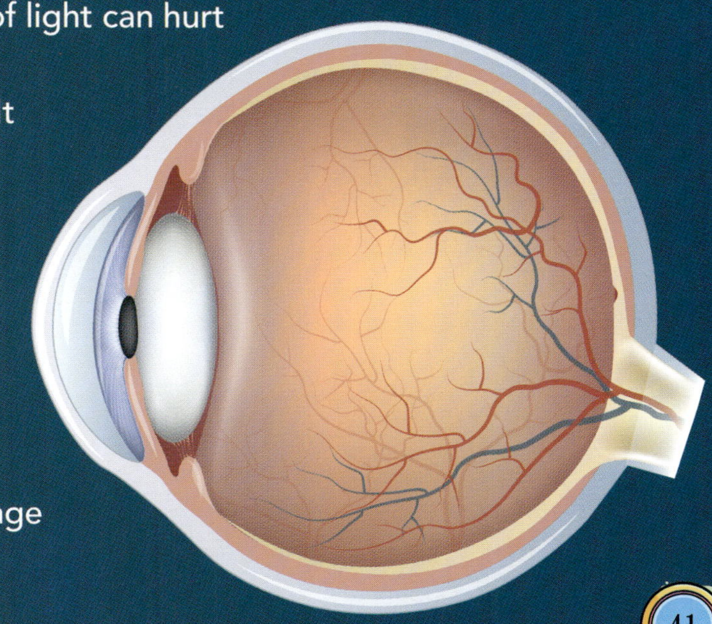

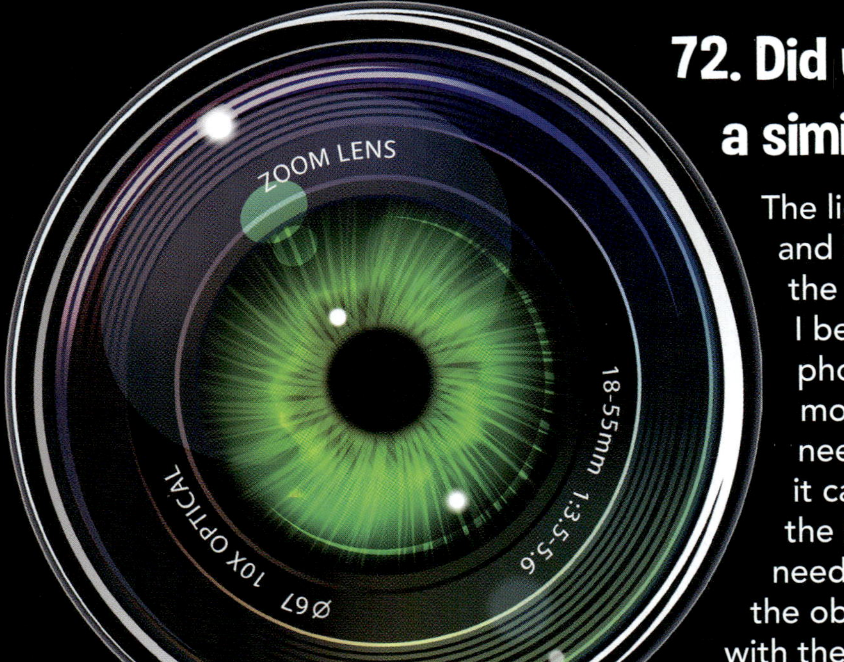

72. Did you know our eyes work in a similar way to a camera?

The light passes through the lens of our eye and is 'recorded' on the back of the eye onto the retina. Have you clicked a photograph? I bet you have. Let's say you are clicking a photo of a monkey. What do you do if the monkey jumps to a far away tree? You will need to adjust the lens of the camera so that it can focus clearly on the monkey. Just like the lens of the camera, the lens of the eye needs to adjust itself when the distance from the object changes. It needs to change its shape with the distance so that we can see clearly. When the lens of the eye is not able to change shape or focus clearly, we need to wear glasses.

73. Did you know the image that is formed at the back of retina is upside down?

Yes, that is absolutely true. But why don't we see things upside down as well? Well, it so happens that when the nerves in the retina send the picture to the brain, the brain turns the picture the right way up and we can see things the right way up! This is exactly how a camera takes pictures as well! The picture recorded by the camera is upside down but when you look at the picture as a printed photo or on a computer screen, it is not upside down.

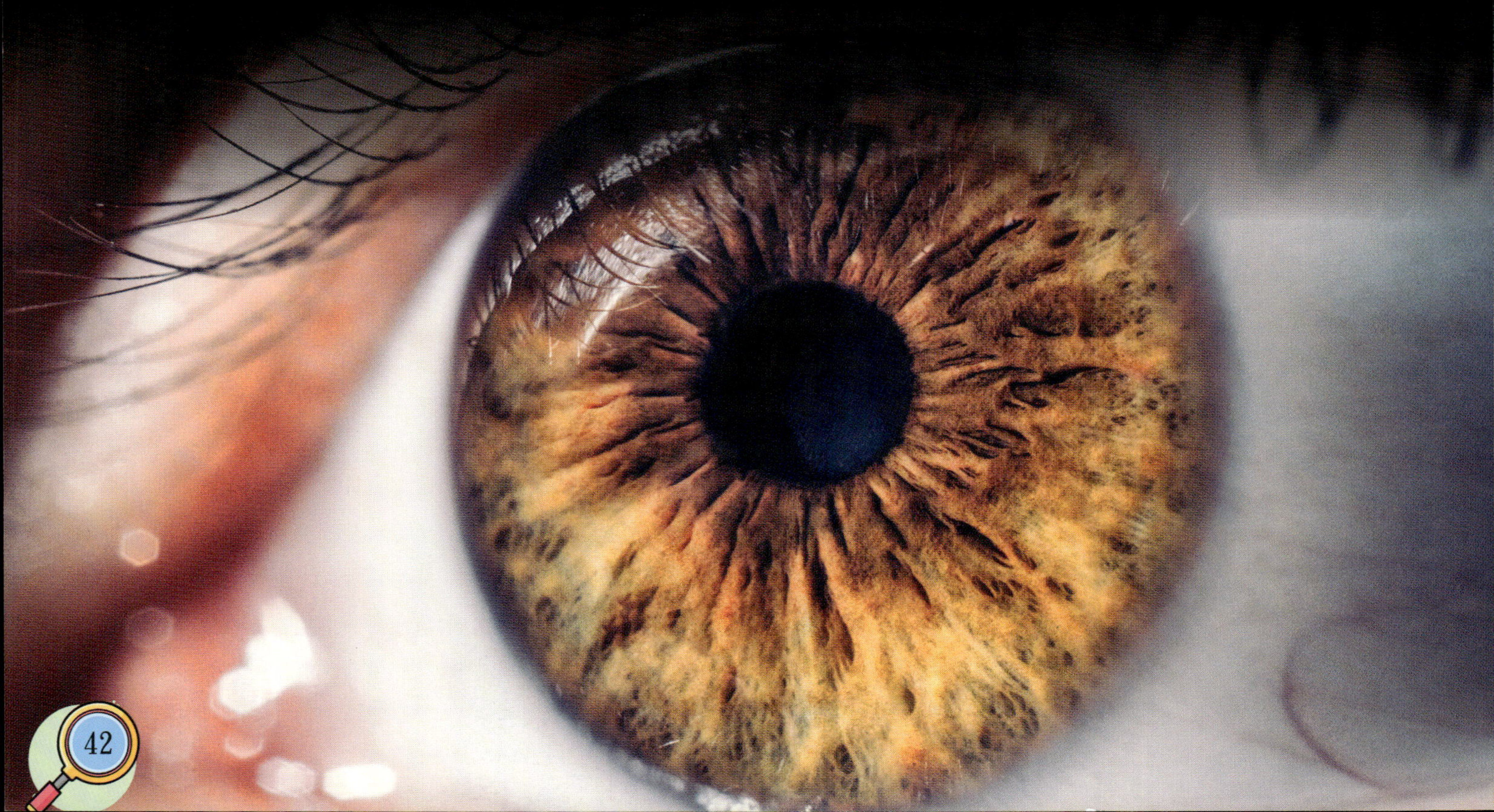

74. Why do our eyes shrink when there is too much of light like on a bright, sunny day? Have you ever felt your eyes relaxed and become normal once you are in shade? Why does it happen?

We know that light enters our eye through a black hole called pupil. It is surrounded by another circle called Iris. Iris controls the size of the pupil. It can make the pupil go smaller or bigger, thus controlling how much light should go into our eye. But how does it all work? Iris is made of a group of tiny muscles. When there is too much light around us, the muscles in the iris shrink. This makes the pupil smaller like a tiny dot so that less light enters the eye. Can you now imagine what will happen if we are in the dark room? In a dark room, the muscles in the iris expand. This makes the pupil go bigger than usual so that more light enters the eye and we can see clearly.

75. Do you know that the hair in our nose helps us to smell?

When we breathe, the air goes into our nostrils. There are many tiny hair inside the nostrils called cilia. We already know about how cilia can trap the germs and dirt and act as our bodyguards. But there is another very important function of cilia. These tiny hair are connected to nerves that send signals to the brain about the smells around us. We smell things when they release small molecules that float in the air. These molecules reach our nostrils and activate the nerves in the cilia which take the information to the brain and we know what we smell. Pretty amazing, isn't it!

But did you know that the sense of smell gets bored easily? When you enter a bakery, you are very aware of the smell at first but by the time you select your favourite cake, you will no longer be able to smell the different smells around you. But it will be refreshed if you give your nose a little break. Go and breathe some fresh air. Try the bakery now. How delicious it smells again!

76. How does the tongue sends messages to the brain to know what we taste?

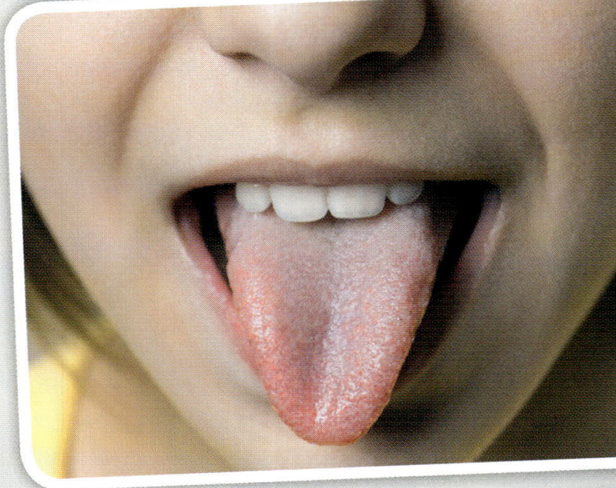

Our tongue is a very interesting organ. It is made up of a group of strong muscles. We know how it moves around the teeth to help us chew and grind. It also helps us to push the food towards the throat so you can swallow it. It also helps us to speak and make different sounds. Hey, why don't you speak all the alphabet out loud? Feel how your tongue rolls to let you say some of these! But how does it help us to taste the food? Our tongue as well as the roof of the mouth is covered with many, tiny bumps called taste buds. Chemicals in the food activate the nerves in the taste buds. These nerves then send messages to the brain and we know what we taste. Taste buds can taste different flavours - sweet, sour, salty, bitter and even the combination of these flavours. Who likes chocolates? It is both sweet and bitter.

77. My food doesn't seem to have much flavour when my nose is stuffy or when I have cold. Why is that so?

Well, it's because the senses of nose and tongue work together to create the true flavour of the food. In fact, most of the taste comes from the sense of smell. That is why our food is not as tasty when we have cold. So what is exactly going on here? While we chew our food, the chemicals inside the food not only activate the nerves in the taste buds but also those present in the cilia of the nose. Don't believe this? Try holding your nose the next time you eat something. You'll observe that your taste buds are able to tell your brain something about what you're eating, perhaps that it is sweet or salty but not the exact flavour until you let go of your nose.

78. Can you guess which is the busiest organ in our body?

Do you think it's your eyes or perhaps your hands?

No, that is not true! Think and think hard! Perhaps it is the organ that is making you think right now? Yes, it's your brain. It is working even while you are sleeping. It is like a super computer that controls each and every thing we ever do. Just like a computer it downloads, processes and reacts to the flood of information it receives. It can do so with the help of billions of nerves reaching out to it from every organ of our body. We are able to think, learn, create, feel emotions, breathe, blink, sleep and even dream because of our brain.

79. What does our brain look like?

Our brain is made up of pinkish gray wrinkled tissue and is about the size of a large grapefruit. Do you want to know how it feels like? Do you imagine it to be as hard as a walnut? Absolutely not! It is very soft and squishy, kind of like tofu. Unlike a cut or some scraped skin or broken bones that can be healed or mended, our brain cannot repair itself. That is why the brain is safely tucked inside a thick, hard skull.

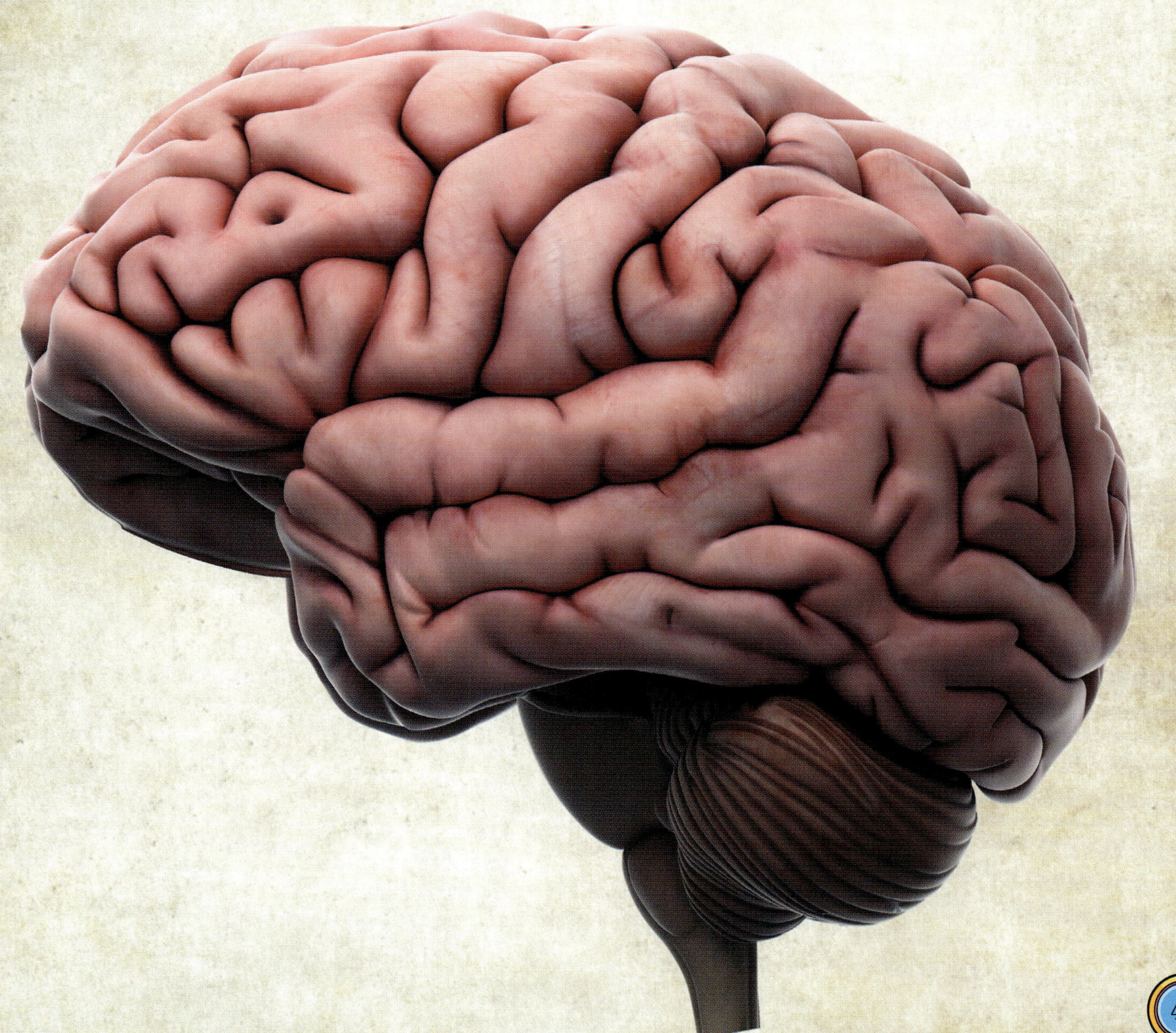

80. Do you know that our brain is divided into two parts and each part has its unique functions?

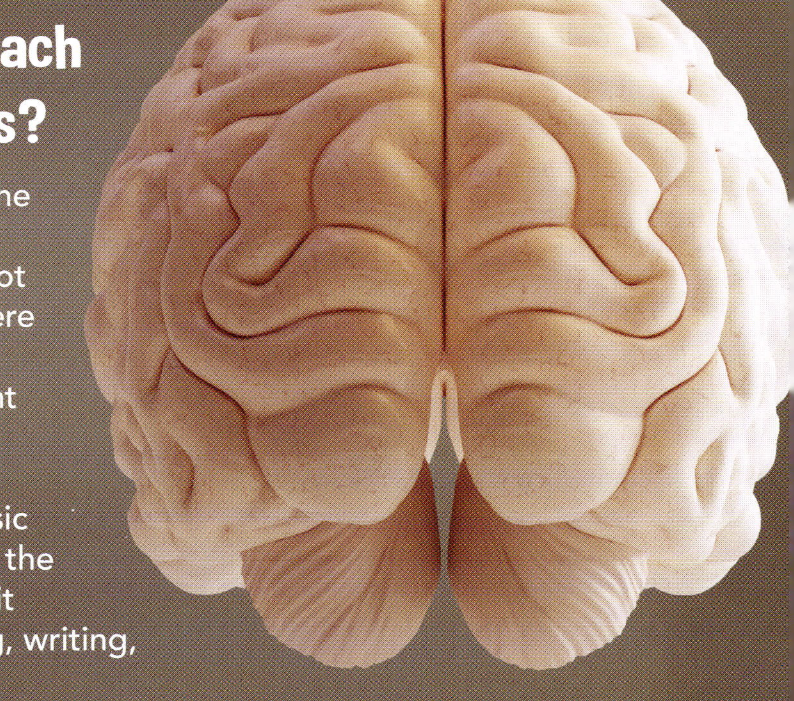

Our brain is divided into two hemispheres, the left and right. Although equal in size, these two hemispheres are not the same and do not carry out the same functions. Each hemisphere is responsible for different functions and behaviours. The right hemisphere or the right brain is often called the creative side of the brain. It is responsible for functions such as face recognition, imagination, creativity, music ability and intuitions. The left hemisphere or the left brain is the logical side of the brain and it controls language, speech, listening, reading, writing, mathematical calculations and memories.

81. Do you know it's our brain that makes us right-handed or left-handed?

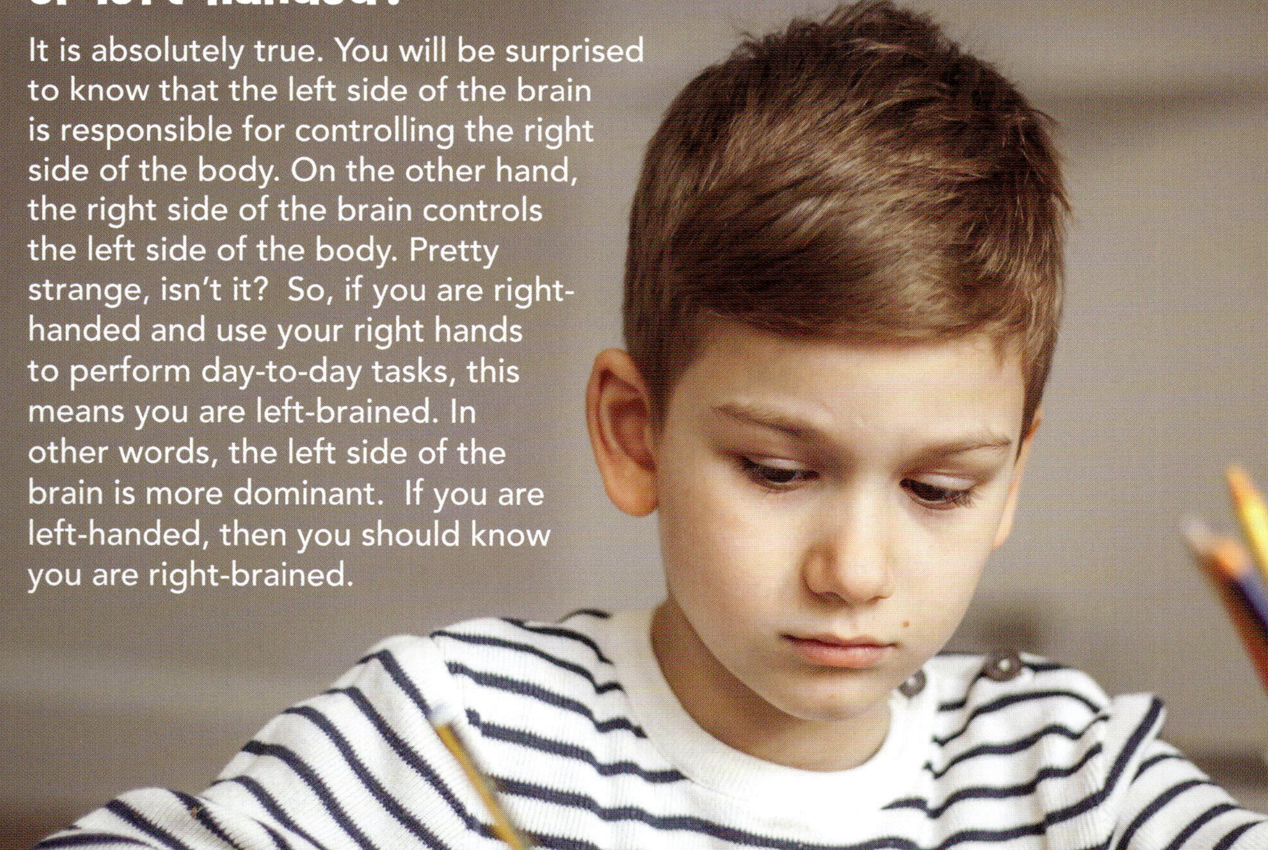

It is absolutely true. You will be surprised to know that the left side of the brain is responsible for controlling the right side of the body. On the other hand, the right side of the brain controls the left side of the body. Pretty strange, isn't it? So, if you are right-handed and use your right hands to perform day-to-day tasks, this means you are left-brained. In other words, the left side of the brain is more dominant. If you are left-handed, then you should know you are right-brained.

82. Why do we have belly button?

When a baby is growing inside its mother, it can't breathe or eat food on its own. Instead, it gets the oxygen and the nutrition from the mother through a tube. This tube is connected to the baby's belly and is known as the umbilical cord. After the baby is born, it can breathe and feed on its own. So, the doctor cuts the umbilical cord and a tiny stump is left. This stump falls off after a few weeks and the baby is left with a belly button.

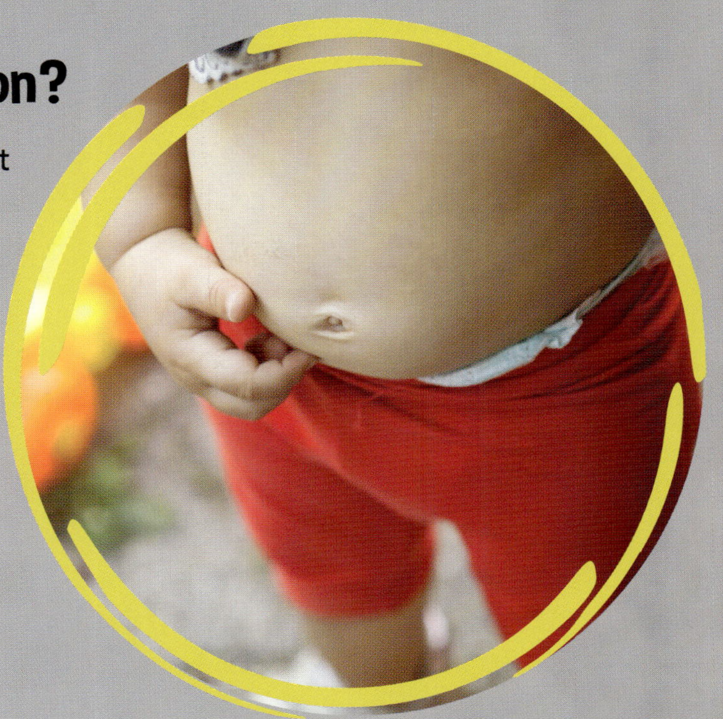

83. Why do our hands have lines in them?

Think of all the amazing things our hands can do! They can bend, stretch, wiggle and wave! To be able to do all that, the skin that covers our hands should be able to adjust to the changing shapes. Try to bend your fingers or close your hand to form a fist. Can you see how these lines help fold the skin around this area? That is the reason we have these lines. We develop these lines in the mother's womb itself, before we are even born. They're technically called flexion creases.

84. Can anyone in the world have same fingerprints as yours?

No. There are no two people in the world who can have the same fingerprints. In fact, even each finger in your hand has a different print. Take prints of your two fingers and compare. You will see a difference in the pattern of your fingers. This is the reason why fingerprints are an important evidence in solving crimes. Fingerprints begin to develop right when the baby is in the womb of the mother!

85. When you cut your finger accidently, it hurts. Then why doesn't it hurt to cut our hair?

Well, you don't feel any pain when you cut your hair because the hair that shows above your scalp is made up of dead cells. However, at the scalp, their roots are attached to the nerves. Nerves are little messengers inside our body that tell the brain what we feel such as pain, hot or cold. That is why when someone pulls your hair, the hair is tugged at the roots and you feel pain. It is the same reason why it doesn't hurt to cut our nails from the top. If you try to cut the nail too close to the skin, it will cause pain because our skin has many nerves.

86. You have just eaten something and you burp. You drink some fizzy drink and you burp. What makes us burp?

Burping is the way in which our body gets rid of extra air. When you eat and open your mouth, you swallow some air too. You don't want this air to go inside your tummy, do you? You throw this air out by burping. There is another way our body gets rid of extra air. Can you guess it? Yes, we fart.

You know when an astronaut burps in the outer space, some food particles may also come out. They call it a wet burp! Yuck!

87. Why do we fart?

Now, that is a very smelly question. We fart when we pass the gas out from our body. How do we get this gas? Our body digests the food we eat with the help of good bacteria present in the stomach and intestines. As these bacteria work on the food in our intestines, they release gas that has sulphur in it. Sulphur has a smell that is similar to rotten eggs. Our body gets rid of this excess gas by passing it out. And that's when it makes a funny sound.

See, how our body makes funny sounds like sneezing, burping, and farting!

88. Have you ever noticed wrinkles on your grandpa or grandma's face, around their eyes and forehead? How do they get there?

When we are young, our skin produces a large number of proteins called collagen and elastin. They make our skin stretchy and elastic just like a rubber-band! So, when you make an expression, for example, a smile, your skin gets stretched around your lips but it simply snaps back into place when you stop smiling. The skin also has a better ability to hold moisture when we are young, making it soft and supple. As we get older, our bodies produce less collagen making it less stretchy. It also loses the ability to hold moisture and makes the skin dry. The creases or the lines have a tough time snapping back into place and they just stay there, creating a wrinkle! Apart from old age, over - exposure to sun rays and pollution also cause wrinkles to occur before time.

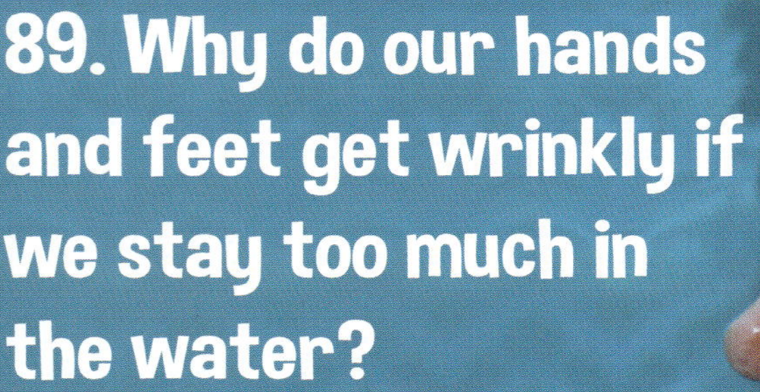

89. Why do our hands and feet get wrinkly if we stay too much in the water?

Sometimes, after getting out of the bath, our fingers, and toes shrivel up like prunes. Even though we can't see it, our skin is covered with special oil called sebum. Sebum moisturises and protects our skin. It also makes the skin a little waterproof. That's why water simply runs off our skin, instead of getting absorbed. But if we stay in water for too long, sebum gets washed away. The water thus goes inside the skin and makes it wrinkly.

90. Why do old people grow white hair?

The roots of our hair contain a number of pigment cells. These pigment cells produce a chemical that gives colour to our hair. When we grow older, our body stops producing this chemical so, our hair starts to become gray or white in colour. The chemical that gives colour to our hair is called melanin. Infact, there are two types of melanin found in the hair—dark and light. They blend together in various proportions to make up a wide range of hair colours. That's why we see people with black, brown, red and blond hair.

If we grow white hair with age, how come some young people also have white hair? Well, it seems there are other factors that can make our hair grow white sooner. Exposure to pollution and frequent use of harsh chemicals such as hair dyes and strong shampoos can make our hair white too.

91. Why do some people have darker skin than others?

The cells in our skin produce melanin that gives colour to the skin. So, if the pigment cells in your skin make more melanin, you will have a dark skin colour. In the same way one will have fair skin colour if less melanin is produced by the skin. But what makes some skins to produce more melanin than others? It is because melanin has another purpose too. It absorbs the harmful ultraviolet (UV) rays of the sun. So, people living in hotter climates make more melanin to protect their skin. People living in colder climates don't need this protection, so they make less melanin and have fair skin colour. But there is another factor that decides our skin colour. It is our genes!

92. Why do we apply sunscreen?

If we are out in the sun for longer periods, our skin can dry up as it loses moisture. It can cause wrinkles to appear on our skin. Moreover, some parts of the sun rays, called UV rays, are harmful to the skin and can cause skin diseases. Melanin is not enough to protect our skin from these rays. Fortunately, we can protect our skin by applying sunscreen. It is made up of a mix of chemicals that shield our skin from the strong sun rays. It doesn't block the rays altogether but limits the number of rays that go inside our bodies. Sunscreen is available as sprays, creams, gels, and lotions.

93. If sun rays are harmful, then why does mom ask us to play in the sun?

Our skin makes vitamin D when it is exposed to the sun. This vitamin is very important for making our bones strong and healthy. We don't need to be in the sun for too long as our body needs only a few minutes of sunlight every day to make this vitamin. Sun is the closest to the earth during noontime and this is when the sun rays are strongest. So, morning time or late in the afternoon sounds a good idea to have fun in the sun!

94. Do you know we tend to be happier and more energetic on a sunny day?

It is because sunshine boosts the production of a special chemical in our body that makes us happy. Yes, our body produces different chemicals known as hormones. Hormones are made by special glands in our body and are passed into our blood. The most important function of the hormones is to make sure that all the body organs are working together smoothly. Hormones have huge effect on how our body responds to situations of tension, danger and happiness.

95. What are genes?

Have you ever wondered why people often remark that you look like your mom or dad or grandfather or even some distant uncle? How can one person look similar to another person in the family? Well, it is because each of us carries a secret code in our bodies. These codes have a lot of information on our physical appearance and sometimes even the special skills that we are going to possess such as artistic skills etc. Your parents pass these codes on to you through genes. Each cell in our body contains thousands of genes.

So where did your parents get their genes from? Of course, from their parents! So when you inherit your genes, it is not only from your parents but also from their ancestors. There is no wonder then if you look like your grandfather! It is all in the genes after all!

And genes aren't just in humans. All animals and plants have genes, too.

96. Do we inherit the genes from both the mother and the father?

Absolutely. Have you noticed that your hair is brown just like father but you have freckles like mom? It is because you inherit traits from both your parents. So how does it happen? Genes are strung on long strands called chromosomes. Chromosomes exist in a pair. One half of the chromosome comes from the mother and the other half from the father. So you get some genes from your mom while some from your father. There is a gene for everything in your body. For example, there is a gene for eye colour, skin colour, height, shape of the nose, ear and even how your personality will shape up. Humans have at least 30,000 genes and 46 chromosomes in total.

Interestingly, goldfish have more genes than humans!

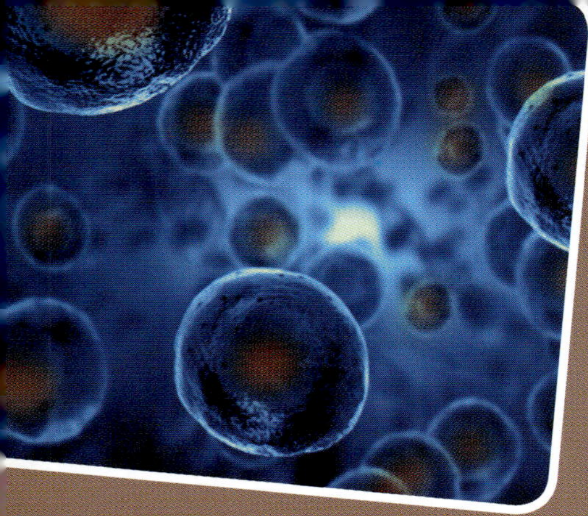

97. What are cells?

Cells are the building blocks of everything around us. Yes, everything! All the living and non-living things are made of cells. Complicated? Okay, let's understand! What is your house made up of? Yes, bricks. So bricks are the building blocks of the house. So many bricks make a house. In the same way, so many cells join together to make different things.

98. Why do onions make us cry?

Ever seen your parents crying when they chop onions? They're not sad; the onion is making them cry! This is how it happens. Onions contain some natural chemicals. When you slice an onion, these chemicals are released into the air and these get in your eyes. This makes your eyes sting and tears come out of your eyes. The harsh chemicals in an onion contain sulphur. It is sulphur which is responsible for this stinging action. Sulphur has a very strange and sharp smell. It is found in everyday items such as in fireworks, paints, detergents, egg yolk and in some medicines too.

99. Why do eggs turn hard after they're boiled?

Have you ever cracked an egg? You must have seen a gooey white liquid gushing out along a squishy round yellow yolk in the middle. So, why does this liquid turn into something solid and rubbery when you boil the egg in the water? It has something to do with what eggs are made of. Eggs are made of lots of proteins and that's why we eat them. This protein is held together by strings or chains of amino acids through a bond. When heated, this bond becomes stronger and the protein changes its form, making the egg hard.

100. How do doors at some shopping stores open automatically when you stand in front of them?

It is so because of the amazing technology of sensors. And what does a sensor do? It senses things around it. It can sense a change in sound or light around it. It can also detect if something has passed by it. Depending on the needs of the device, different types of sensors are made to detect different things. In shopping stores and also in some office buildings, the sensor in the door is made to detect things like weight, light, and movement. And when it does sense these things, it sends the signal to open the door on its own. Does it sound familiar to you? This is how the nerves in our body work. They sense things around us and send the signals to the brain!

101. Why does a candle flame extinguish when we blow it?

You all must have blown candles on your birthday. When you blow, the flame extinguishes and everyone claps and sings the Happy Birthday song for you. Well, let's understand first how a candle burns. The candle needs two things to burn - fuel and oxygen. A candle uses wax called paraffin wax as fuel to burn. When you burn the candle, the wax turns into liquid and gets mixed with the wick or the thread-like thing you see in the candle. The liquid then evaporates as wax vapour and keeps the flame alive. When you blow, the candle gets cool and the wax can no longer evaporate. This means the wick no longer gets the fuel and the flame extinguishes. When you blow a candle, you must have seen white rings of smoke. They are the wax vapours evaporating into the air. There is another thing. A candle needs oxygen to burn. When we blow, the oxygen supply is shut. The flame feels suffocated and dies!

102. What is a barcode? How does it work?

A Bracode has parallel lines, black and white Lines have different width. Some are thin and some are thick There is a number mentioned just below the lines.

Each line on the barcode means a number. This code or number is already fed into the software of a computer. So when the cashier scans the barcode, it shows the item matching the code and tells the price of the item. This way the supermarkets can work with much more speed and ease.

103. What is toothpaste made of?

Water - It doesn't let the toothpaste get dry.

Abrasives - These are chemicals that keep your teeth clean. Use a toothpaste with gentle abrasive.

Fluorides - They are chemicals that prevent tooth decay.

Surfactants - These detergents help in making foam.

Flavour - Mint is the most common flavour but there are others.

Preservatives - Prevents. microorganisms from growing in the toothpaste.

Sweeteners - Are added to improve the taste of the toothpaste.

Colouring agents - These are added in coloured toothpastes.

104. Can a shark lose all its teeth and never eat again?

When our milk teeth break, we get our permanent teeth. After that, if our teeth break, they don't grow again. But if a shark loses teeth, they can grow back again and again. A shark can re-grow upto 20,000 teeth in its lifetime! Yes! But we get the chance once.

105. Are turtles cousins of tortoise?

Yes. They both belong to the same family. But a turtle lives in the water while a tortoise lives on land. They are similar in many ways. But there are some differences as well. Let us see what they are:

A tortoise has a heavier shell than a turtle.

A turtle eats both plants and animals but a tortoise only eats plants.

It is believed that the longest living turtle was 86 years old but the longest living tortoise lived for 326 years! That means that the tortoise has a longer life span than turtles.

106. Why is a jellyfish called a jellyfish?

A jellyfish has no bones. It is soft like the jelly you eat. So that is why it is called a jellyfish. Jellyfish can be red, pink or orange! Just like the way you can make your jelly in different colours! A jelly fish may look very beautiful but it is very dangerous. Her tentacles have stinging cells that paralyse other fish and animals before she eats them up. They can sting even when they are dead! They like to eat shrimp, crabs and small plants.

Jellyfish are bad swimmers and depend on the ocean current to swim. They digest their food very quickly, otherwise carrying undigested food for a long time doesn't help them to swim.

107. Is starfish a fish?

No. A starfish is not a fish. It doesn't have fins like other fish. It has tube-like feet to swim. Fish have gills to breathe but a starfish doesn't have gills. They breathe through their feet. Their feet have thin tissues that circulate oxygen from the seawater into their bodies.

A starfish can shed or drop its arm if a predator attacks it. It takes some time like may be a year for the arm to grow back. This helps the starfish to protect itself. They also have spines on their bodies to protect themselves. Their eyes are tiny red spots at the end of the arm.

108. Can blue whales talk?

Yes. Blue whales can talk as well as sing. They can communicate with other whales far away in the ocean.

Interestingly, the blue whale is the largest animal on earth, bigger even than the dinosaur!

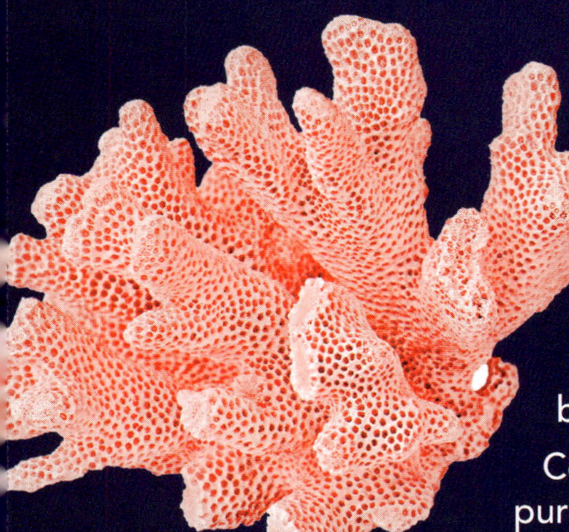

109. What are corals?

What do you think are corals? Are they rocks?

Corals are not rocks. They are actually animals! Yes, they breathe! Corals are tiny little animals called polyps. Thousands of polyps live together to form a colony called coral reef. As polyps die, they become hard and new polyps grow on top of them. This way the coral reef keeps growing big. Many fish make their homes in the coral reef.

Corals can be in different shapes and different colours like purple, pink, white, etc.

110. What will you call an octopus that has seven arms?

Ha!ha!ha!...Good joke. But an octopus can never have seven arms. It will always have eight arms. Guess why? Because when an octopus loses his arm, he can grow it back!

There are many animals like the octopus who can grow their claws or their legs or their tails back. Can you name some?

Lizards, Crabs, Starfish.

Find out more animals like them.

111. Do crabs live on land or in water?

Crabs do not have lungs. They have gills like any other fish which helps them to breathe oxygen from water. But they can live on land for a long period of time, as long as they can keep their gills wet. The water on the gills absorbs oxygen from the air and helps crab to breathe even when it is not in the water. That is why crabs live in cool places on land so their gills don't dry fast.

112. Are dolphins fish?

Dolphins are not fish. They are mammals, the most intelligent and playful. This means they give birth to babies, nurse them and feed milk to their babies. Dolphins breathe air through lungs. They can stay underwater for around 15 minutes and then they need to come up to breathe air.

Dolphins are very social animals. They live in groups of 10-12 dolphins. That is why dolphin shows around the world are so liked by children and adults!

113. How do they train dolphins so well?

Isn't it amazing to see the dolphins jump, flip, dance on their tail and do all kinds of tricks? But how do you train a dolphin? Let's see how.

Trainers use various tools and techniques. But most importantly, they use 'positive reinforcement'. Just like when you behave or perform well, your parents give you a reward in the form of a gift or appreciate you. Similarly, when a dolphin flips correctly, the trainer blows a whistle. The dolphin knows she has done the correct movement and comes to take the reward which may be a toy, a rub-down, trainer's affection or a fish.

To make them jump to a certain height, trainers use targets that can be in the form of a pole. They first set the level of the pole low and gradually increase the height. With time, the dolphin learns how to jump over a height!

114. Why is pufferfish called by this name?

Pufferfish is very interesting. It swims very slowly and looks pretty clumsy while swimming. That is why many fish can easily attack and eat it. Now here is the good part. A pufferfish can puff itself with water or air. Which means it swallows water or air and become many times bigger than its normal size. That is why it is called a pufferfish. This way, it becomes a big ball that is inedible. Some puffer fish have spines that also help them to protect themselves from other animals. Pufferfish also has tetrodotoxin that makes it foul - tasting and poisonous for other animals.

115. What is common between a walrus and an otter?

Both Walrus and Otter are very social animals. They literally 'dance', do 'somersault' and live together in large numbers. If you see them sleeping, they would sleep like a large family, all huddled together! They chirp, tap, squeal, scream, and make all kinds of noises. They live in cold regions near water and ice. Looks like not only human beings love to be among friends!

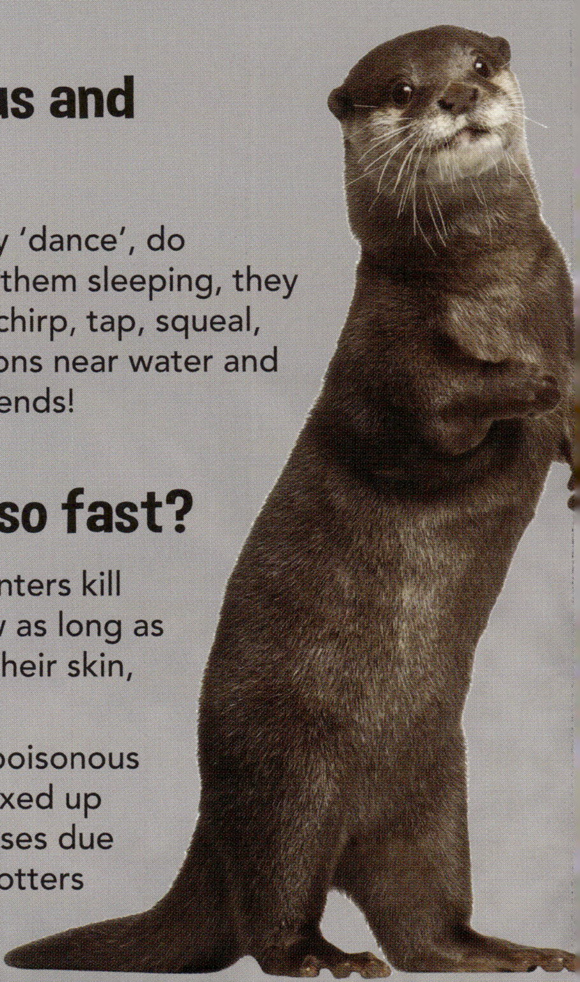

116. Why are walrus and otter dying so fast?

Walrus have teeth called tusks which are very precious. Hunters kill walruses for their ivory tusks. Their teeth or tusks can grow as long as 3 feet. The tusks grow throughout their life. Besides that, their skin, oil and meat are also sought after.

Otters are dying rapidly because of pollution. The oil and poisonous substances are being thrown in the rivers and these get mixed up with the oceans. These poisonous substances spread diseases due to which otters are dying. There are many animals like the otters that are dying due to pollution in the water bodies.

117. Why is it said that you change colours like a chameleon?

A chameleon can change its colour according to its surroundings. This ability is called camouflage. So when a chameleon sits on a leaf, it turns green. When it is on the trunk of a tree, he becomes brown. It does so to protect itself from any attack by other animals. This way it merges with the surroundings and no one can spot it. Since a chameleon can change its colour anytime, people who change when the situation changes for their own safety are often referred to as chameleons!

There are many other animals who can camouflage like seahorse and octopus. Can you find out some more names?

118. Is seahorse really a horse?

No. A sea horse resembles a horse. That is why it is called a sea horse. There is nothing else common between the two. In fact, a horse runs very fast but a sea horse can hardly swim. It swims very slow! A sea horse lives in corals. It can change its shape and colour according to the coral he lives in to protect itself from other animals. You know by now that when any animal changes its colour according to the surroundings, it is called camouflage. Now, that is something a horse cannot do!

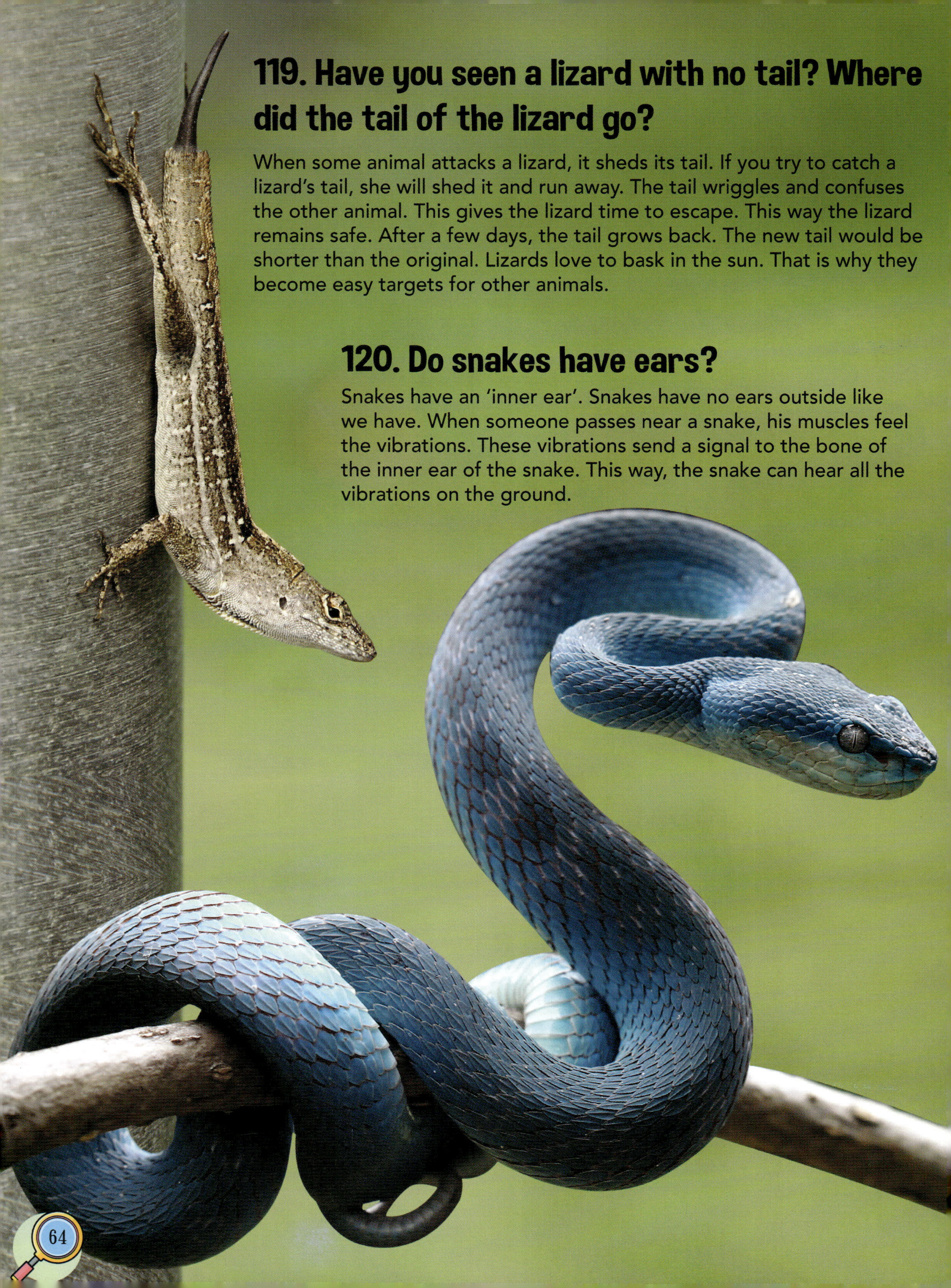

119. Have you seen a lizard with no tail? Where did the tail of the lizard go?

When some animal attacks a lizard, it sheds its tail. If you try to catch a lizard's tail, she will shed it and run away. The tail wriggles and confuses the other animal. This gives the lizard time to escape. This way the lizard remains safe. After a few days, the tail grows back. The new tail would be shorter than the original. Lizards love to bask in the sun. That is why they become easy targets for other animals.

120. Do snakes have ears?

Snakes have an 'inner ear'. Snakes have no ears outside like we have. When someone passes near a snake, his muscles feel the vibrations. These vibrations send a signal to the bone of the inner ear of the snake. This way, the snake can hear all the vibrations on the ground.

121. Like Spiderman, the squirrels can run on electric wires, climb up and down the trees. Why don't they fall?

Squirrels are not Spiderman but these furry animals are very energetic. Yes, they can climb trees and wires with ease because:

They have razor-sharp claws to hold the tree and run up and down, hang and even jump from one tree to another!

They have flexible joints to move around quickly.

They have padded feet that don't let them get hurt even if they fall from a height of 100 feet.

Squirrels are cute but they can be a big problem! They have very sharp teeth which they use to cut things, even the wires of your house!

122. How can a flamingo stand on one foot and not feel tired?

Have you ever seen flamingos on a lake? If you have read any story about flamingos, the most common way of showing a flamingo is standing on one leg! Imagine, if you had to stand on one leg all the time, won't you feel tired? Let's find out the secret why flamingos don't get tired.

The flamingo is sleeping while standing on one leg! Do you find it strange? Now read more. Only half of the flamingo is actually asleep. Half of the flamingos that has one leg standing is active. The flamingo then takes a turn. It swaps over and then the other leg takes rest.

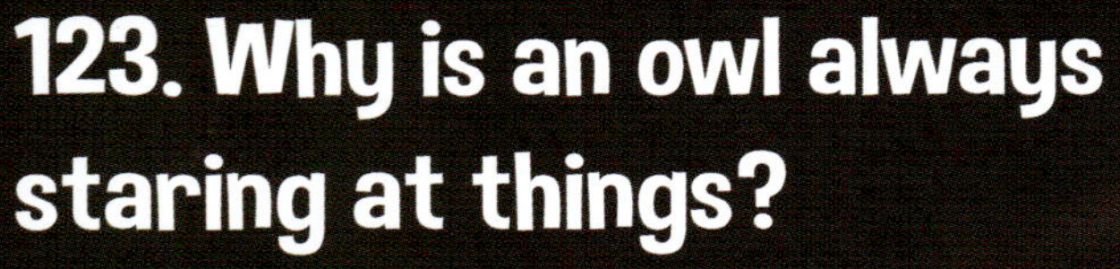

123. Why is an owl always staring at things?

An owl looks very funny. He seems to be constantly staring at something. But the fact is that an owl cannot move his eyeballs like we can! Yes, to look left or right, an owl has to turn his neck and then see. So, he is often found sitting in one position, looking straight.

124. A porcupine has thorns around his body. Why?

These thorns are called quills. These quills are like knives of a porcupine. The moment an animal attacks a porcupine, the quills get inside the animal's body. Ouch! It must be really painful to have sharp needle-like quills get pricked into your body. This way the porcupine protects itself. The porcupine grows its quills again and again. That means he never runs out of his knives. Normally, the quills are lying down. But when a porcupine senses danger, they stand up. Observe the hair on your arms when you are scared. They will stand up too!

125. Penguins are black and white. How do they know who is who?

Every penguin has a distinct voice. So when they call each other, they recognise the voice and know who is calling. In fact, when mother and father penguin go for fishing, they leave their children in crèche. A crèche is like a large group that stays together and waits until the parents return. So when the parents come back, they call out for their children. They immediately recognise each other's voices. Then, the parents feed the young children with fish and shrimps! What a feast!

126. Even a zebra is all black and white. They all look alike. So how do you differ?

Well, here you are wrong. Every zebra may be black and white but each zebra has a different pattern of stripes. For human beings, it may be very confusing but zebras know the difference. Then, of course, there are two more ways they recognise each other. Zebras recognise each other from their smell and sound. This helps them know who is who!

127. Are polar bears really white in colour?

A polar bear is always seen as white but its real colour is black. It has a layer of black fur under the white fur.

Why do you think there is a layer of white fur on the top? Ok, let's see! A polar bear lives in the Arctic which is full of snow.

The double layer of fur keeps the polar bear warm in cold.

The white fur helps the bear to blend (camouflage) with the white snow. And why do you think the polar bear would want to blend with the snow? It helps the polar bear to protect himself from predators.

128. Why do camels have a hump?

Tick the right answer -

- To store water
- To store food

So that people can hold and don't fall when they ride a camel

It absorbs all the heat of the desert so that the camel doesn't feel too hot.

The right answer is option (b). A camel stores fat in its hump. The fat comes from the food it eats. When there is less food, the camel uses this fat to get energy. This way he can live for days in the desert without food.

129. All the plants in a desert are thorny and hard. Then, what does a camel eat?

A camel has thick lips. These help the camel to eat anything. They can eat bitter, hard, thorny plants! If a camel is hungry, it can even eat leather shoes! So beware!

Green plants also provide water to the camel. Having thick lips is a way of adapting (adjusting) to the hot, dry climate of the desert. That is why camels have large, puffy feet that help them to walk on sand. There is also a double layer of eyelashes so that the sand doesn't get into their eyes. They can also close their nostrils if there is a sandstorm!

130. How long does a kangaroo live in the pouch of his mother?

A baby kangaroo is as small as the size of a grape! It cannot swallow or suckle like a normal baby. The mother kangaroo uses her muscles to put the milk down the throat of the baby. The mother keeps it warm and safe in her pouch.

Baby kangaroo is called a joey. When a joey is 4 months old, he leaves the pouch for some time to eat shrubs and grass. But after some time, he returns to his mother's pouch. When he is ten months old, he is mature enough to leave his mother's pouch and hop around in the forest on his own!

131. Are there other animals like kangaroo?

Animals that carry their babies in outside pouches are referred to as marsupials. There are many animals who raise their babies in the pouch-like the sugar glider, the koala bear and the possum.

Usually, mothers carry the baby inside their body for a few weeks and when the baby comes out, he is fully developed. Of course, the baby needs the care but his body parts are all developed. He no longer needs to suck the mother's milk.

132. Why is koala always sitting on the trees?

It is quite a sight to see a koala wrapped around a tree like a teddy bear! Koalas live on trees and they love to sleep. Koalas can sleep for as long as 20 hours continuously! Their soft fur acts like a cushion. So they comfortably hug a tree and sleep merrily!

Koalas have sharp claws that help them to climb up the trees. They also have a sharp sense of smell. They smell the eucalyptus leaves and eat the ones that are the best! Looks like that a koala lives the life of a king sitting upon the tree!

133. Which animal has the largest mouth?

Hippopotamus! Have you ever seen him open his mouth? Did you notice his long canines! His sharp, long teeth that can cut a boat into two will scare you away! Also remember when a hippopotamus 'yawns', it doesn't mean he is tired. It is a sign of aggressive behaviour!

Hippos love to stay in the water. Their eyes and nose are right on top of their heads. That's why their whole body can stay in the water while the eyes and the nose remain above the surface of the water.

134. Is it true that a mouse has teeth so sharp that it can cut the net?

It is absolutely true! A mouse can even bite into wood!

Rats and mice eat grains, insects and even wood. They eat as much as 20 times a day! These small creatures are more active at night and eat after every few minutes. Not only that, they can jump from great heights without getting hurt. So don't underestimate them because they are small!

135. Is an elephant's trunk its nose or its mouth?

The trunk is an elephant's nose. He uses his trunk to lift things. Where elephants work as helpers, they use their trunks to lift logs of wood or to push them aside. In the circus, they would pick up a hat or a ring or even the clown! He uses his trunk to fill it with water and drink. An elephant also fills up his trunk to splash water on his body when he is feeling hot or needs to itch. If you ever get to observe an elephant, see him pick up bananas and eat. They would literally peel the banana with their trunk and take it to the mouth to gulp it down!

136. Which animal can climb trees, can swim and stand and sit upright?

A bear! Yes, a bear can walk straight like a human being. They also have sharp claws because of which they can climb trees.

Bears are omnivorous—they eat both flesh and leaves. Bears who live near water love salmon. Bears that live in cold climates hibernate for a long time. They go to sleep and don't wake up at all, not even to get any food. Asiatic bear who lives in a warm climate doesn't hibernate at all.

Bears howl, jump and can be scary when angry. But strangely no animal attacks them except for themselves! A male bear may attack his own cubs. That is why the mother bear is protective and may attack the male bear.

137. Why do frogs croak?

You must have often heard that unmelodious song of the frogs, especially at night. It is called croaking. Why do you think frogs croak?

Male frogs croak to attract females. But there is another reason also. Croaking means they are establishing their territory and are warning other male frogs to find some other place. Have you noticed that frogs croak more in rains? There is no clear answer on this. Some say that frogs anticipate rains and since they love moisture, they get excited and croak. While others say that mating season begins for them during rains, so they croak more to attract females!

138. How does a hummingbird sing?

A hummingbird cannot sing! She flaps her wings continuously (almost 80 times per second). The flapping makes a humming sound. That's why it is called a hummingbird!

The hummingbirds have fast breathing rates, fast heartbeat, and high body temperature because of which they eat often. As they flap their wings at such a fast rate, they spend a lot of energy. That is why they eat after every few minutes. They eat nectar, insects, and pollen. They have a tube-like bill to suck nectar from the flowers. A hummingbird is the smallest bird in the world. It can weigh just 2 gm!

139. Why do woodpeckers peck wood?

It is a way for them to search for food and a place to make their nest. Woodpeckers also tap to attract mates, to establish territories and also to communicate. Woodpeckers do not have vocal cords, so they drum on objects such as hollow trees and logs, utility poles and chimneys, etc.

140. Is it true that the egg of an ostrich is very big?

Yes. It can weigh up to 1.5 kilograms or 3 pounds. Do you want to feel how heavy this is? (Why don't you ask your parents to give you a packet of sweets or nuts that weigh the same?) The egg of an ostrich is the largest among all animals. Not only that, but an ostrich is also the tallest and the heaviest bird. It can be as tall as 9 feet (Measure your height and also your father's height. Make a total. An ostrich may be taller than you both!) She may weigh up to 350 pounds! That doesn't sound like a bird. She is so heavy and tall that she cannot fly.

141. Is it true that bats cannot see? If they cannot see, then how do they fly around safely without hitting trees and other animals?

It is not true that bats cannot see. They can see but in the dark or at night. To fly around they use a technique called echolocation. Let's divide this word into two parts-echo + location. The echo, as you know, is the sound that returns when you shout. So bats make noises and wait for them to come back. If the sound doesn't hit any object and doesn't come back, it means it is safe for the bat to fly forward. That is how they locate their way. They can also tell from how quickly the sound bounces back that how far an object is!

142. Why do some birds have colourful feathers while some don't?

Which bird would you look at—a brown or a colourful one? Of course, a colourful one! Perhaps, this is the reason why most of the female birds are usually brown or dull-coloured so that when they lay eggs, no one can spot and harm them. While the male birds have colourful feathers called plumage. The red, blue, orange, green shades attract the female birds. This is the way of birds to start a family. Peacocks (males) attract the peahens (the female bird) to become friends with its dance of colourful feathers.

143. Why do birds migrate?

When there are winters and heavy snowfall, the food becomes scarce. The birds then migrate or temporarily move to warmer places. There are a lot of bird sanctuaries around the world where birds get a natural environment. They have the forest and a pond of water so that they can comfortably live there till they wish to. When summers arrive, they go back to their homes. So, it's like a holiday for them!

144. How do babies of birds breathe inside the egg?

The shell of the eggs is porous. That means that it has very tiny holes that are invisible to the eyes. Oxygen from these holes enters an egg and the baby is able to breathe. Air can move in and out of the shell of the egg.

145. How does a baby of the bird eat inside the egg? Are there holes for that also?

No, No. There is no such hole. You must have seen a broken egg. It contains two parts - the yellow portion and the white portion. The yellow portion is called the yolk. The baby bird gets its food from the yolk. The white portion is called albumin. It surrounds the baby inside the egg and protects it from the sudden rise or fall in the temperature.

146. Is there a bird that lays blue eggs?

Robin lays blue-coloured eggs! A pigment called biliverdin gets deposited on the eggshell due to which it has a bright blue colour. The healthier the female robin, the higher the pigment biliverdin and thus brighter the blue colour! Interesting, right?

There are many other interesting facts about the robin that make it different from other birds - It lays eggs mid-morning while most of the birds lay eggs at sunrise. This is so because robin likes to eat a lot of worms and uses the morning hours to hunt for worms.

Robin sits on her eggs for incubation when she has laid all her eggs. Smart move, this way she has to sit on her eggs for 10-12 days once and not again and again.

147. Why do fireflies glow?

There is an enzyme in the tail of the firefly. It reacts with oxygen to cause a chemical reaction. This reaction produces a chemical called Biolumiscence that gives the tail its glow.

Fireflies also called lightning worms or glow worms are actually beetles. They emit light to attract mates and prey and to repel predators. They are usually found in warm areas. In many countries, the coming of fireflies signifies the beginning of Summer!

148. Why do birds sing in the morning?

It would be a good idea to get up early someday and listen to the sounds coming from the trees. If you are living a little away from the city, it is almost like a chorus singing by the birds! Even if you are in the city, you can hear the birds singing. Why do you think birds sing in the morning?

Are they welcoming the sun?

Are they praying to God?

Are they calling to their friends?

Well, there are two reasons. Firstly, male birds sing to attract mates and secondly, they tell the other birds that this is their territory. It is like a warning to other male birds not to enter their area!

149. Why do spiders spin a web?

Spiders eat bugs and insects. What better way to catch bugs than to trap them in a web! So, spiders spin a web to catch their food. How do they spin a web? Spiders produce silk threads to build their webs. The silk threads can be thick or thin, dry or sticky. When the spider begins to make a web, it shoots a silk thread. The thread comes out as liquid, but it dries quickly in the air. The spider anchors this thread to an object such as a doorknob, a tree branch or even to a wall. It then moves to and fro to add more threads to make the web strong and create an interesting pattern. When an insect flies into a spider's web, it gets stuck to the sticky threads!

150. Why doesn't the spider get stuck in the sticky thread itself?

Well, it is because not every strand of a spider's web is sticky. It also uses non-sticky threads in its web. So, when the spider needs to walk across its web, it remembers to put its feet on only the non-sticky strands. This way a spider doesn't get stuck in its own web. But this is not all! There is one other interesting reason for this. Did you know spiders have eight legs? So, if accidentally it steps on to the sticky parts of the web, a spider is able to free itself. It balances on the rest of its legs on the non-sticky strands and pulls the other leg free pretty easily!

151. Why do ants walk in a line?

Ants live together in large colonies. They live together, party together and search for food together! Ants work very hard to bring food. And they bring home food for other ants also!

When ants go in search of food, each ant leaves a chemical behind. The other ant follows the smell of that chemical. That is why they walk behind each other in a line. This way they never get lost!

152. Do you know tiny ants can carry big things?

Like an army of strong workers, tiny ants can be seen carrying pebbles or grains on their heads. The muscles of ants are much stronger than many large animals. They can lift things that are 50 times heavier than their body weight! Now imagine, if hundreds of ants come together and see a chocolate lying on your bedside! They may just lift up your chocolate and carry it to their home for a party!

153. How do honey bees make honey?

Honeybees use nectar in the flowers to make honey. Nectar is a sugary liquid found in flowers. They use their long, tube-like tongues to suck the nectar out of the flowers and they store it in their 'honey stomachs'. Bees actually have two stomachs, their honey stomach which they use to store nectar and their regular stomach.

The honeybees then return to the hive and pass the nectar to the other bees called 'worker bees'. The worker bees suck the nectar from the honeybee's stomach with their mouth. These bees then spread the nectar throughout the honeycombs where water evaporates from it, making it a thicker syrup. The bees make the nectar dry even faster by fanning it with their wings. Once the honey becomes thick, it is ready to be eaten. The honey is stored in the honeycomb until it is eaten.

In one year, a colony of bees eats between 120 and 200 pounds of honey.

154. What is a honeycomb?

A honeycomb is an amazing structure that honey bees build with honey. The honey bees use the honeycomb to lay eggs and store honey. It is also called beeswax and is edible.

A honeycomb is a marvellous piece of creation. Each section of the honeycomb is an exact hexagon with six sides with a precise 120-degree angle for each side. See the picture. Draw a honeycomb and you will know how difficult it is to make each hexagon of the exact same size with the same angle! But the honey bees do it. And you know that they have never gone to a school to learn math!

155. Why do bug bites itch?

Different bugs bite in different ways. When bugs like bees, wasps and ants bite, they inject a chemical or toxin into our skin. This toxin makes us itchy. Sometimes, it can be painful and may cause a small red bump at the site but the good news is that the itchy feeling goes away after a while.

Bugs like mosquitoes leave their saliva on our skin when they bite. This saliva makes us itchy.

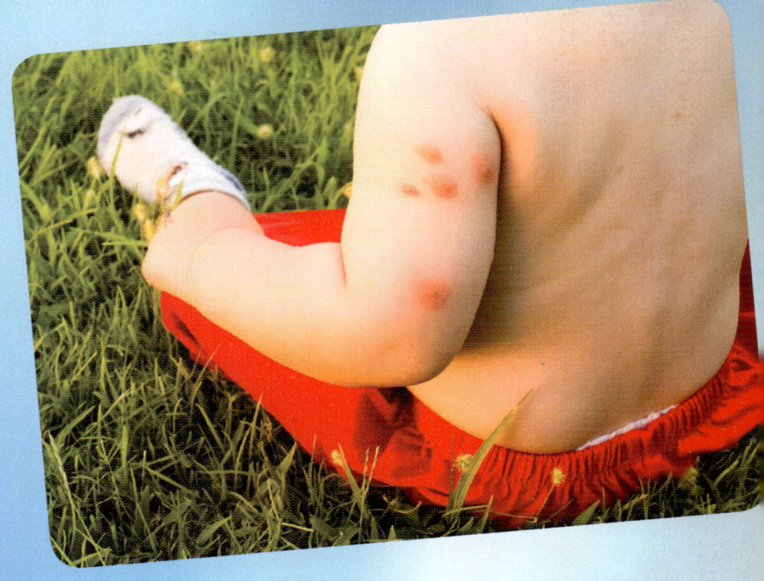

156. Is it true that a mosquito is a very dangerous insect?

Mosquitoes can be very harmful insects. Not only their bite makes our skin itchy, they can cause diseases like malaria and dengue. These diseases can be life-threatening if not treated well in time. In fact some mosquitoes even pass some diseases from one person to another. How does it happen? For example, a person is already infected with a virus. When a mosquito bites this person, it also picks up the virus along with the blood. So, when it bites another person who is healthy, it passes the virus into his blood. Mosquitoes breed on standing water. It takes just a few inches of water for a female to deposit her eggs. So keep your surroundings clean of any standing water!

Did you know only female mosquitoes bite us! The female mosquitoes don't need the blood as their food but to nourish their eggs!

157. If only female mosquitoes bite us then what do males mosquitoes snack on?

You will find it interesting that both male and female mosquitoes feed on nectar and plant juices. In addition to this, female mosquitoes also need protein to develop eggs. This protein is not present in the nectar but is found in our blood. Since male mosquitoes don't lay eggs, they don't need this protein and don't bite us.

158. Why do mosquitoes buzz in our ears?

How many of you have had a sleepless night because mosquitoes kept buzzing in your ears? They seem to never leave until you wave your hand at them. Do you think the buzz is produced by the flapping of their wings? No. In fact, the buzz sound is produced by a tooth-like organ at the base of the wings of a mosquito. This organ scrapes against itself when the wings move and make the buzzing sound. You hear this buzz louder whenever they're close to your ear. Did you know a mosquito's wings move 300-600 times per second?

But what is it that attracts the mosquitoes to your side? It is the carbon dioxide that we exhale from our mouth that is signal to the mosquitoes that their meal is near. Scientists have also found out that the buzz of the mosquitoes is only to annoy you or to detect their victim to suck blood.

159. Why do earthworms come out from the garden and walk around in the driveway when it rains?

Well, earthworms breathe through their skin. Their skin is covered with mucus which has to be moist all the time in order for them to breathe. In the ground, it's all dark and there is no exposure to the sun. So, their skin does not remain dry and they breathe well. During the rains, the environment is all wet and earthworms can survive on the surface. Therefore, the soil loosens up and they come out for a stroll! Earthworms can survive very well in water also as long as there is enough oxygen. So they also don't fear to drown.

160. What are 'crocodile tears'?

A crocodile uses its teeth to grab and crush but not to chew the food. It simply swallows an animal like a turtle or a frog. Its stomach has stones to grind the food. When the crocodile is moving its jaws and when the food is getting grinded in the stomach, its eyes begin to froth and bubble. This results in rolling down of the tears. So, the crocodile cries when he is actually enjoying eating his food! That is why if anybody is shedding fake tears it is said, 'He is shedding crocodile tears'!

161. What do earthworms eat in the ground?

Here you can guess well. They eat the fungi, the bacteria and even the decomposed waste in the soil! The decaying roots and plants are good food for them. The manure we add to the soil is like a feast for them. The remains of animals are another source of food.

All this eating and nibbling at food makes them natural farmers! Yes, millions of earthworms in the soil do the job of ploughing by turning the soil. The tunnels that they make help the soil to get more air, making it more fertile. And don't forget that their poop acts like a fertiliser!

162. When someone acts wildly, why do you say 'Don't act like an ape'?

Some animals have a specific behaviour like some jump a lot, some run very fast while some are plain lazy. Their examples can be used to describe how we behave sometimes too. These examples or expressions are called idioms. 'Don't act like an ape' is one such idiom.

Apes can act really wild when they get angry. So when someone is being loud, aggressive and wild, we use this idiom. There are many types of apes like gorillas and chimpanzees. They have many similarities with human beings. Their features resemble us, they are also very intelligent, they socialise like us and kiss and hug each other to express love.

163. When someone is lying, why do you say, 'He is crying wolf'?

Cry wolf means to cry or complain when nothing actually is wrong. You must have heard of the story where the boy kept raising a false alarm that a wolf had come. He would do this to attract the attention of the villagers. But one day when the wolf actually came, all villagers said, 'Don't listen to him, he is crying wolf'. Nobody came to his help and the wolf ate him away!

164. I have been doing this task for 'Donkey Years'? What does it mean and what has it to do with a donkey?

A donkey is considered to be a hard-working animal. He is talked in stories as an animal that can do a task over and over again. He can carry a heavy load and cannot do anything that requires a brain. So, in a way he is an animal who works hard but is not too intelligent.

So when someone has been doing a task for many years, he says I have been doing it for donkey years. It also shows that since he has been doing the task for such a long time, he knows it very well. When you do a task many times, does it require much intelligence? No, right? So that's why the comparison to a donkey.

165. I am not doing any monkey business. I am very fair in my work. What kind of business is 'Monkey Business'?

Again, have you read stories about a monkey? What kind of character is he portrayed as? Cheat, cunning, clever, liar, right!

So, whenever anybody uses unfair or wrong methods to do a task or run a business, it is said he is running a monkey business. When you talk about a dishonest person, you can say he is into monkey business. Have you ever lied to your mother? If you have, then I must say you should stop the monkey business! Honesty always pays.

Can you think of more such idioms where they talk about some animal? Like 'holy cow', 'raining cats and dogs'. Find out such idioms and also why they use example of that animal.

166. Why is it said that the police and the thief are playing 'a game of Cat and Mouse'?

You must have seen 'Tom and Jerry'. What is happening in the cartoon all the time? Tom, the cat, is trying to catch Jerry, the mouse, right? So, whenever someone is trying to catch someone like a friend or even a thief, it is said they are playing cat and mouse.

It means to find someone who is hiding from you.

167. Why do police use dogs as part of their team to find thieves?

Dogs are considered to be loyal, watchful and protective animals. That is why they are the most popular pets. Because of these qualities, they also form an important part of the team of police. They are trained extensively and can help to solve a difficult case.

Dogs help to sniff the whereabouts of a thief which normally a policeman cannot know.

Dogs help to find out illegal drugs or explosives because of their strong sense of smell.

They can be great guards till the policeman is away. If the thief tries to act smart, they can bark and even chase the thief till the policeman returns and puts him in jail!

168. Global warming! Why is it such a big deal? After all, we all like to be a little warm and cozy, don't we?

Our planet Earth is special. It has the right environment and the right temperature that makes it liveable. It is true that different places in the world have different temperatures. Some are too hot while some are extremely cold but the average temperature of the Earth makes it fit to live on. There are some important gases in the Earth's atmosphere that naturally help the Earth to maintain the warmth it needs. These gases are called greenhouse gases. These gases absorb some of the Sun's heat and keep the Earth warm.

But what would happen if more greenhouse gases are released? More greenhouse gases will mean more heat will be trapped. This will make the Earth warmer than usual. This is called global warming.

169. Why are more greenhouse gases being released?

Carbon dioxide and methane are some examples of greenhouse gases. Though they are naturally present in the Earth's atmosphere in small amounts, some man-made activities release more greenhouse gases.

We use fossil fuels such as petrol and coal to produce energy. When we burn these fuels, carbon dioxide is released.

Smoke coming out from factories contains these gases too.

Trees absorb some of these harmful gases and turn it into fresh oxygen. For example, trees absorb carbon dioxide and give out oxygen. When we cut down trees to make paper, shopping malls, houses, and factories, it leads to the accumulation of carbon dioxide in the air around us.

170. But how exactly can the rise in Earth's temperature harm us?

The increase in the Earth's temperature or global warming is causing many unnatural things to happen.

With the increase in temperature, the natural habitats of plants and animals are changing faster than they can adapt. Since it becomes difficult to cope up with the changing environment so quickly, some species of plants and animals are dying or becoming endangered.

Glaciers are melting due to the rise in temperature. As the water from the glaciers finally goes into the sea, the sea levels are rising. The areas near the sea are in danger of getting drowned. The sudden changes in weather also lead to disasters like cyclones, earthquakes and tsunamis.

171. What are the glaciers and where are they found?

Glaciers are huge masses of ice. They can only form in places where more snowfalls in the winter than it melts in the summer. Then the snow starts to stack up! When you look at them, you may think they are lying still but glaciers are constantly moving. There are many glaciers all over the globe. Glaciers form high in the mountains or at the North Pole and the South Pole where it is extremely cold. The biggest glaciers are found in Greenland (near the North Pole) and Antarctica (in the South Pole).

Global warming is making these glaciers melt at an unnatural speed. Scientists are worried that if glaciers start to melt too much, it would cause huge floods. It will lead to drowning or submerging of areas that are situated near the sea. Do you know that at Glacier National Park in West Glacier, Montana, there were 150 glaciers in 1850! But today this number has reduced to only 26.

172. Is there any way we can control global warming?

Here is a list of things we can do to help:

Save Fuel use: If the place you are going to is close enough, ask your parents or guardians to walk or take a bike instead of taking out the car.

Carpool is another wonderful idea to save fuel. If people living in one area have to go to the same place every day and at the same time such as school, office or library, you should try to carpool.

Recycle: We can recycle plastics and paper. Don't waste paper. Take a print out from the computer only when it is very necessary.

Plant more trees.

173. What are fossil fuels?

What do you imagine when you think of fossils? Perhaps the first thing that comes to our mind is the bones of prehistoric animals that used to live on the Earth some millions of years ago. Over a period of time, the remains of these animals and also plants were covered with many layers of mud, dirt and rocks. These layers created heat and exerted pressure over these dead parts, converting them into fossil fuels.

Fossil fuels are buried very deep under the earth and sometimes even under the ocean floors. Scientists and engineers explore areas around the world to find out sites rich in fossil fuels. They have special instruments and devices that help them study rock samples from an area. It gives them some reading and tells them if the site has fossil fuels and is good to drill. Engineers drill down with special machines to collect this fuel.

174. Why is it not a good idea to use fossil fuels excessively?

Firstly, burning these fuels releases harmful gases like carbon dioxide in the atmosphere. Secondly, it takes more than millions of years for nature to make these fossil fuels. If the oil we use today took millions of years to make, what do you think will happen if we run out? It will take another million years to make it. That is why these are called non-renewable sources of energy. It means they can get finished if they are used too much.

In fact, we have other sources of energy around us that will neither run out nor produce pollution. Do you know what these are? These are other natural sources of energy that will not be finished even if we use them excessively. They are called renewable sources. Sun, wind, rain-water and waves are examples of renewable sources of energy. It means they will never run out no matter how much we use them! What's more, they are clean and absolutely free! But how are they used?

175. How is energy from the Sun converted into electricity?

Sunlight is used to make solar energy. You have been using solar energy every day; to dry your clothes in the Sun and to warm up in winters. But it can also be used to make electricity. All we need to catch are some sun rays with the help of solar panels. How does it all work? The solar panel has solar cells. These cells contain a special metal called silicon which helps to convert the Sun's energy into electricity. In a solar power plant, many solar panels are used to catch solar energy. This energy is used to heat water into steam. The steam turns the big turbines and produces electricity.

176. What is silicon?

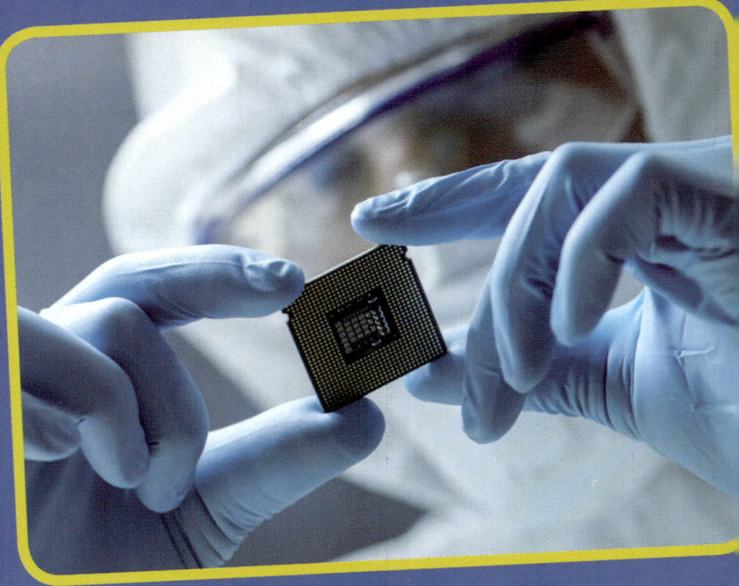

Silicon is found in so many things around you. It's in the cement; it is in your computer, televisions, video game consoles and even in your mobile phones! Are you wondering where this silicon comes from? Silicon is found on the beaches in the form of sand. Silicon obtained from just one ton of sand can produce as much electricity as burning 500,000 tons of coal. But we don't use silicon on a large scale yet as it is expensive and solar cells require silicon of high purity. Scientists around the world are trying to design solar cells that can use low purity silicon and can be effective too. Scientists are also researching on other materials that are less expensive and can be used to make solar cells on a large scale.

Just think how much cleaner the environment would be if we can prevent burning of huge quantities of coal?

177. Wind power can be used in a number of ways. Can you think of any?

Ok, how do sailboats move? You got it! They use the power of the wind to sail through the water. This energy can also be generated with wind turbines. In fact, one wind turbine can produce enough electricity to power around 300 homes. Now, a wind turbine works exactly the opposite of how a fan works. Instead of using electricity to make wind, a turbine uses the wind to make electricity. Let's see how. They have 3 blades which can move very fast. Wind pushes turbine blades so that they rotate very fast. The rotating blades turn a generator to convert this energy into electricity. Large groups of wind turbines are called wind farms.

Do you know sometimes these blades rotate over 200 miles per hour! The wind turbines can be 200 m high! It is because of their height that if something goes wrong, rock climbers are hired to repair them.

178. SAY NO TO PLASTIC BAGS! We have seen people campaigning on roads, in shopping malls and on T.V. Why are plastic bags so bad?

Plastic bags are not nature-friendly. Whenever we throw something as waste, small insects and microorganisms attack it and try to break it into smaller pieces. They either eat it up or turn it into something useful that helps nature. For example, if you will throw food peels or leaves, the tiny creatures will either eat it up or turn it into a gloop (slime/paste) full of nutrients. This gloop goes back to the soil and helps to grow healthy plants. But not all things we throw are nature-friendly, for example, plastic. Microorganisms are not able to break plastic things into smaller pieces. So, it keeps on lying there and harms nature.

179. How does plastic harm nature?

When we throw the used plastic bags on land, it hinders the absorption of water by the soil and makes it less fertile.

Land animals might eat it along with grass or other food items lying on the ground. It can choke them or get stuck in their stomach, making them very sick.

When we throw plastic in the water, it can harm water animals too if they eat it.

Since plastic floats on the water surface, it blocks the sunlight to reach the water animals and plants. It can make them all die without sunlight!

180. What about paper that we use every day, such as, paper bags and newspapers? Are they bio-degradable or nature-friendly?

Yes, the paper is bio-degradable. It means that microorganisms are able to break it down and it goes back to nature without harming it. So, is it okay to use as much paper as we want? No, we should not use it unnecessarily. We should not waste paper as it is made from wood. Lots of trees need to be cut to make paper. Trees give us oxygen to breathe and food to eat.

We should not throw away the used paper in the garbage. Instead, you can save old newspapers and drawing sheets to make creative things such as a paper tree, paper animals, paper dolls and so much more! You can also collect all the old and used paper and take it to a recycling centre.

181. How is paper made from wood?

To make paper, trees are cut down into smaller pieces like chips or cornflakes. Yes. It is lot of hard work! These chips are then made into a gooey pulp (imagine something like orange pulp, though not as tasty!). This wood pulp is then poured over a large screen, where it is pressed and dried to create thin sheets of paper! Paper is used to make storybooks, drawing sheets, notebooks and newspapers!

182. What is recycling? How can we recycle paper?

Recycle means turning old and used things like paper into new products. There are special factories that make recycled goods. And the good news is it takes less energy for these factories to make these products. This would mean less air pollution. So, what else can be recycled? Almost everything we see around us can be recycled such as plastic, batteries, clothes, glass, electronics and much more. If we use recycled products, we don't have to make new plastic or new paper. It will come from what we already have. It will also mean that we will have less garbage on the Earth lying around that can harm nature.

183. What happens to all the garbage that we throw away every day? Where does it go?

The trash collector takes all the garbage to a special place called a landfill. A landfill is a large hole where all this garbage is dumped. This garbage keeps on lying there and takes so much space. After all, we throw away so much garbage every day, don't we? So, recycling seems a good idea. As we will reuse most of our old things with recycling, we will have less garbage to throw and less garbage will go to the landfills. Have you seen a landfill near your home? Well, a landfill is usually built very far away from places where people live. We would not like to live near a stinking place after all!

184. There is so much water on Earth. Why should we not waste water?

We have big oceans and so many rivers. So, what is the big deal in using as much water as we want without worrying too much about it? Well, all the water on the Earth is not fit for use. Water in the oceans is salty and we cannot drink or cook in it. So, most of the water that we use comes from under the ground. Streams, rivers and lakes also hold freshwater.

Do you know nature recycles this water in its special way? It does so by making rain. Rain replaces and refills water that we use but it takes time to do that. Do you think it rains every day? No, it doesn't. So, if we keep on using water and waste it, it will not get refilled quickly by nature and we will have no water when we need it.

185. How are clouds made?

Clouds are made of tiny droplets of water or ice crystals. You must be aware that water is found in three forms: Solid (Ice), Liquid (Water) and Gas (Water vapour) and these forms can be interchanged. It happens like this:

When you keep some water in the refrigerator, it cools down and turns into ice. It is called freezing.

When ice turns into the water due to heat, it is called melting.

When water is heated further, it turns into water vapour. It is called evaporation.

When water vapour cools down, it turns back into water and it is called condensation.

Let's see now how clouds are made. The heat from the sun makes the water from rivers, lakes or oceans to become water vapours. The water vapours rise into the sky where the air is cooler. Now, the cool air cannot hold as much water vapour as warm air. So, the extra water vapour has to go somewhere. The water vapour gets condensed onto tiny pieces of dust particles floating in the air, forming ice crystals around them. When billions of these tiny ice crystals come together they form a cloud.

186. You must have noticed how grown-ups often refer to the weather forecasts before planning an outdoor activity such as a picnic or a journey. Have you ever wondered who makes these forecasts and how?

There are special scientists who study Earth's atmosphere and predict what the weather would be like in the coming days or even how it might change in the hours to come. These scientists are called Meteorologists. They use tools to help them find out how the weather is shaping up. They study clouds and winds. They also use satellites, aircraft, ships and hot air balloons to observe the atmosphere. From all these studies, they collect the data they need to predict the weather. In fact, it is not just the weather, they also use this data to alert us about the coming hurricanes, tornadoes, tsunamis, snowstorms, so that we can be prepared in advance for these natural disasters.

187. Why does the water vapour form droplets around a dust particle?

It seems quite strange but the air has to be just a little bit dirty for clouds to form. It is because water vapour needs a surface to condense onto. Even the cleanest air has some particles of dust, smoke or salt. The water vapours cling to these particles and form water droplets and even ice crystals. And why does a cloud float? The droplets are so small and light that they can float in the air. When the droplets keep growing, they become so heavy that they can't stay floating in the cloud and fall as rain! Sometimes the water droplets in the rain freeze before they reach the ground and become hail, sleet or snow! It is known as precipitation.

188. What do you see when you look at clouds? Do you see puffy balls of cotton or is it some strange animal shape you see? Why are there so many kinds of clouds?

There are many types of clouds. Each type of cloud is formed in a different way with its unique shape and bringing its own kind of weather. No two clouds are alike. The shape of a cloud depends on the conditions in which it is formed, such as temperature, wind and height. All these conditions decide if the cloud comes out looking wispy, puffy, feathery, lumpy or like a flat sheet. For example, depending on the height (altitude) at which the clouds are formed; they are classified as low level, mid-level and high-level clouds.

189. What are the different types of clouds? What do they tell us about the coming weather?

The shape of the clouds and the height at which they are found can tell us a great deal about the coming weather. Let's look at the most basic type of clouds:

Stratus clouds: These are usually flat and look like layered sheets. They are low-level clouds, formed at around 6500 feet. These clouds often cover the entire sky with a dull-gray colour and produce only drizzle.

Cumulus clouds: These are puffy clouds that look like cauliflower. They are also low-level clouds. But these clouds can grow upwards and develop into huge cumulonimbus clouds, which are also called thunderstorm clouds.

Cirrus clouds: These are thin and wispy clouds formed at high altitudes. They are made up of ice crystals. Although few cirrus clouds mostly indicate clear weather but an increased cover means that a change in the weather is coming.

We know that all clouds don't produce rain. Weather scientists have given a special name to the clouds that rain. It is called Nimbus.

190. We have seen white clouds and even grey ones. But do you know there are green clouds too?

What usually happens is that when sunlight hits a cloud, the water droplets in the clouds reflect all the visible colours of this light, making the cloud look white. The green colour in the cloud is not completely understood but it is believed that it occurs when there are a large amount of water droplets and hail inside the clouds. This makes the cloud scatter the light in such a way that it reflects back only green light, making the cloud appear green. Green clouds are mostly linked to bad weather. So if you see a green cloud it is very much possible that heavy rain, hail, severe thunderstorm or tornado is approaching.

191. Do you want to explore the other interesting cloud formations?

Mammatus clouds are huge bulges that hang down from cumulonimbus clouds. They usually mean bad weather is fast approaching.

Lenticular clouds are made by the wave-like wind pattern created by the mountains. They look like discs or flying saucers that form near mountains. Now, this is really cool! If you spot a UFO near the mountains, you will know what that can be, right?

Nacreous or Mother of pearl clouds are quite rare but very beautiful, bright, shining clouds. They look like rainbows and are mostly visible within two hours after sunset or before dawn.

192. Do you know fog is a type of cloud too?

Yes, it actually is. Fog is a stratus type of cloud that is formed very close to the ground instead of up in the sky. It is formed when the air near the ground becomes very cool. So, what happens to the cool air? Since it can't hold much of the water vapour, it condenses into water droplets, thus forming clouds near the ground itself. It is called fog. So, you see how it is formed exactly the same way a cloud is formed. The only difference is the height at which they are formed.

193. Some airplanes, such as jets, leave a big white stripe in the sky while flying. It looks like cloud but is not shaped like one. So, what exactly is this big, trailing stripe?

These white stripes trailing behind a jet are called contrails. Like cars, jets need fuel to fly. When the jet engine burns this fuel, smoke, steam and other chemicals escape from the exhaust of the engine into the sky. When the hot steam from the jet's exhaust gets mixed with the cold air high up in the sky, white stripes of clouds or contrails are formed as the jet moves along. So you see they are made the same way as the clouds but instead of made in a natural way they are made by flying jets.

194. It's not that only jets can make artificial clouds. Clouds can also be made through a process called cloud seeding. Do you know how?

Have you seen a grown up planting seeds in the garden to grow plants? In the same way, clouds can also be grown by seeding with chemicals to produce rain! It all started when scientists thought it will be great if it was possible to produce rains in areas where it didn't rain much. They knew that not all clouds rain. It only rains when there are too many water droplets or ice crystals in the cloud which makes it heavy. So, what do you think they planned to do? They thought it would be a good idea to make the clouds heavy. They planted a chemical inside a cloud that helped to grow more drops and ice crystals and it actually worked.

Cloud seeding is most commonly done through airplanes. Planes fly into selected clouds and release packets that contain very small particles of a chemical called silver iodide. When the particles meet cool moisture in the clouds, they trigger the formation of ice crystals and raindrops.

195. Why do we see rainbows in the sky sometimes? How are they formed?

Sometimes we spot a beautiful rainbow in the sky! Have you noticed that we only see a rainbow when the sun is shining and it is raining simultaneously? Or maybe after it has just stopped raining? This is the time when there are many water droplets present in the air. Sunlight is actually white light and is made up of all the colours of the rainbow. As sunlight passes through these water droplets, it bends slightly and breaks up into the seven colours of the rainbow. Do you remember what do we call the bending of light? It is called refraction.

We see the rainbow as an arch of seven colours.

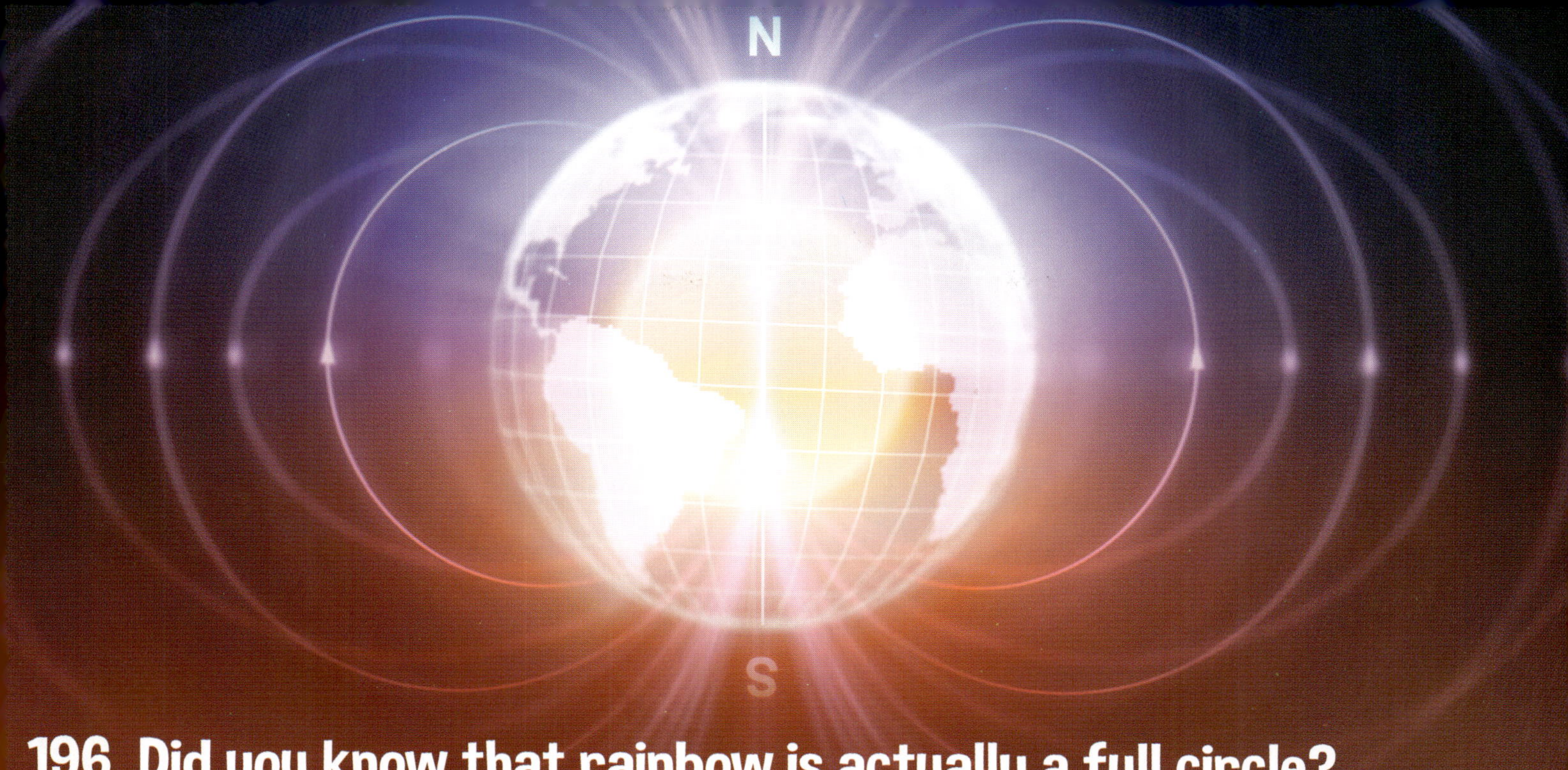

196. Did you know that rainbow is actually a full circle?

Though we see the rainbow as an arch, the funny thing, it's actually a circle. It's just that we don't see the other half as we cannot see the water droplets in the air below the earth's horizon. As we move to higher grounds, the arc of the rainbow gets higher as well. It is possible to view the rainbow from an airplane as well! From there it looks like a complete circle as you can see the water drops which are below the horizon as well as those above it. What's more, you will also see the shadow of the airplane in the centre!

197. Did you know you can only see a rainbow if the sun is behind you and the rain or water droplets are in front?

And what's more, the sun has to be low in the sky to make a rainbow. This is why rainbows are more common in mornings and evenings. It is rare to find a rainbow in the afternoon. Is it possible to see rainbows at night? You must be thinking how that is possible when there is no sunlight. But the fact is, it is very much possible to see a rainbow at night. It happens when moonlight passes through the water droplets instead of the sunlight. These are called moonbows. We don't get to see the moonbows very often as moonlight is not always very bright except on a full moon day.

198. What are the seven colours in the rainbow?

The seven colours are Violet, Indigo, Blue, Green, Yellow, Orange and Red.

How will you remember these many colours?

Psst!

There is a have a magic word that you must be aware of!. It will help you remember the seven colours in the rainbow. It is VIBGYOR and it stands for:

V Violet

I Indigo

B Blue

G Green

Y Yellow

O Orange

R Red

199. What's your favourite colour? Perhaps it is yellow or is it pink? Oh, but there are so many beautiful colours to choose from after all! So, why do we see so many colours around us? Have you ever wondered what makes the sky blue or the grass green? Let's find out!

We see colours because of the light! A beam of white light may look invisible but it is actually made up of all the colours. And every colour has its own unique energy. Red light has its unique energy while green has its own. So, we can say light is actually made up of different types of energy, right?

When light falls on any object, the object absorbs some of these energies and leaves the others. The unabsorbed energies are then reflected back. It is this reflected energy that we see in the form of a colour. For example, a red apple absorbs all the energies except one that belongs to the colour red. It reflects back this energy to the human eye. The eye receives the reflected energy as red light and sends a message to the brain that the apple is red.

200. Why do scientists say black colour is no colour at all?

Actually, a black object appears black because it absorbs all the energies present in the light around it. In this case, what do you think it is reflecting back? It is nothing actually. So, the object appears black.

Let's look at a white shirt now. You see a colour because it is reflected back to our eyes. Since white is made up of all the colours, it means a white shirt is not absorbing any energy or colour from the light around it. It is in fact reflecting back all the colours, appearing white.

201. Can you now think of why grownups suggest that we wear white or light-coloured clothes in summers while black or dark in winters? Does it really matter?

When an object absorbs energy from the light around it, the energy is usually converted into heat in the object. Since white clothes do not absorb any energy, no heat is generated. This makes the white clothes cooler. But if you wear black cloth, it will absorb all of the light energy; therefore trapping some heat.

202. Red, yellow and blue are the three primary colours. Why are only these colours called primary colours?

Primary colours mean they are the main colours and by mixing these, secondary colours can be created. For example,

Red and yellow make orange.

Blue and yellow make green.

Red and blue make purple.

So, orange, green and purple are secondary colours. You can make more colours by mixing primary and secondary colours. Together, these give a whole range of beautiful colours and many shades. So, why don't you try mixing red (primary colour) and green (secondary colour), and see for yourself what colour turns out? Color wheel, which was invented by Isaac Newton shows what shades can be obtained by mixing colours with each other.

203. How do our eyes help us to see and identify colours?

Our eyes have a special organ that helps us to see colours. It is the retina. The retina in our eye has two kinds of receptors— cones and rods. They are also called photoreceptors. It is the cones that help us to see and identify colours. These cones contain colour sensing pigments. While cones help us to see colours, they only work well in bright light. This means we cannot see colours in the dark.

We have three types of cones; red, blue and green. These three kinds of cones help us see all the colours made by mixing these colours together.

204. Why can't we see colours in dark or dim light?

There is another type of receptor in our eyes that helps us to see in dim light and it is called a rod. Though rods catch the light and tell your brain that you saw something, they are not built to see very well. Unlike cones, the rods do not contain colour sensing pigments. They only let us see white and black. This is the reason we don't see colours in very dim light or in the dark. Human beings are colour blind at night.

Did you know that in dim light you can see more clearly out of the side of your eye? It is because rods are located more towards the side rather than the centre in the back of the eye. So, next time you're out on a clear night, try to observe how you can see objects better out of the corner of your eye than from the centre. Isn't this fun?

205. Do animals see colours?

Although there's no way to truly know if animals actually see colours, scientists have examined the cones inside their eyes and guessed what colours they might see. There are special tests to figure this out. The results from these tests and many experiments have shown that animals can see colours. But different animals have different kinds of colour vision. While some animals can't see many colours and have poor colour vision, some animals have amazing colour vision. They can even see colours that are not detected by the human eyes.

206. Are there actually colours that we can't see?

Yes, this is true! There is a part of light whose colours are not visible to the human eyes. It is called ultraviolet (UV) light. Scientists have found that birds have four types of cones. This helps them to detect UV light. This is why birds can see a lot more colours than humans. In addition to this, the colour sensing pigments in their cones are much stronger than humans. This makes the birds see more shades of the same colour. Recent studies show that some fish and turtles too have four types of cones, helping them to see UV light as well!

207. What about cats and dogs? Do they see colours too?

Many animals, such as cats and dogs, have only two kinds of cones in their eyes. In addition to this, the colour-sensing pigment in their cones is weak. Therefore, they probably see very few colours. Neither can they see vibrant shades like we can. But both cats and dogs have a better vision at night. Wondering what colours your pet dog might see? Studies show that dogs see the world around them as yellow, blue, and gray.

208. Why do night birds, such as owls, see better at night?

Owls are nocturnal birds. This means they are most active at night rather than in the day. So, they need to hunt their food at the night. Do you know what owls eat? They eat mice and other rodents which are also active at night. Owls have good vision at night. It is because they have more rods and not as many cones. This makes them lose their ability to see colours but they definitely see a lot better at night. Also, their eyes are very large in comparison to their body size, so they pick up a lot of light rays. Wondering what we call birds that are active in the day? They are called diurnal birds.

Do you want to know a real fun fact on owls? A group of owls is called a parliament. Now that's quite funny!

209. What is colour blindness?

Humans are colourblind at night. But there are people who cannot differentiate between certain colours even during the day. They suffer from a condition called colour blindness. Most colourblind people are able to see things and colours as clearly as other people but they are unable to fully see red, green or blue light. You would be amazed to know that all babies are born colourblind. In fact, a newborn baby sees very little and concentrates mostly on objects very close to him. All of what he sees comes in three basic colour combinations - black, white and shades of gray. His vision improves in a few weeks and he is able to see colours as well.

Did you know bulls are colourblind? They chase the red cape because it is moving, not because it is red!

210. How does a magnifying glass work?

Have you ever looked at an ant through a magnifying glass? The ant looks bigger than what it actually is. Sounds like magic, isn't it? But this is how a magnifying glass works. It makes an object look bigger. It has a glass or a lens which lets you see the image of an object through it. When the light passes through this glass, it bends. This bends the size of the image too and things look bigger.

The silly mirrors in funhouse bend your image so that parts of you look bigger, giving you a silly balloon-head or a long Pinocchio like nose!!

But a magnifying glass cannot make extremely small things visible to us, for example, dust particles or germs that make us sick. For this, we will need a special instrument that has more power than a magnifying glass to make things bigger so that we can see them. What can that be? It is a microscope.

211. How does a microscope work?

The microscope works through the same logic as a magnifying glass. It has a much more powerful lens that bends the size of an object many times over. It makes even the smallest of the small objects to look bigger. The number of times a microscope will make an image bigger is usually written on the side of the microscope. If it says 20x then the image you will see will be 20 times larger than it actually is! If it says 50x then it's 50 times bigger! Now that sounds really exciting!

212. How are we able to look at things in space?

We use the telescope to look at the stars and planets in the sky. Telescope is a long tube with two ends. If you look through one end, it allows you to look at objects that are far away at the other end. The special lens in the telescope can make the far away things stretch-out so that they are big enough for us to see. Thanks to telescopes, we have been able to discover so many planets and stars in the space. But you should remember never to look directly at the Sun as this can cause permanent damage to your eyes due to the brightness of the Sun.

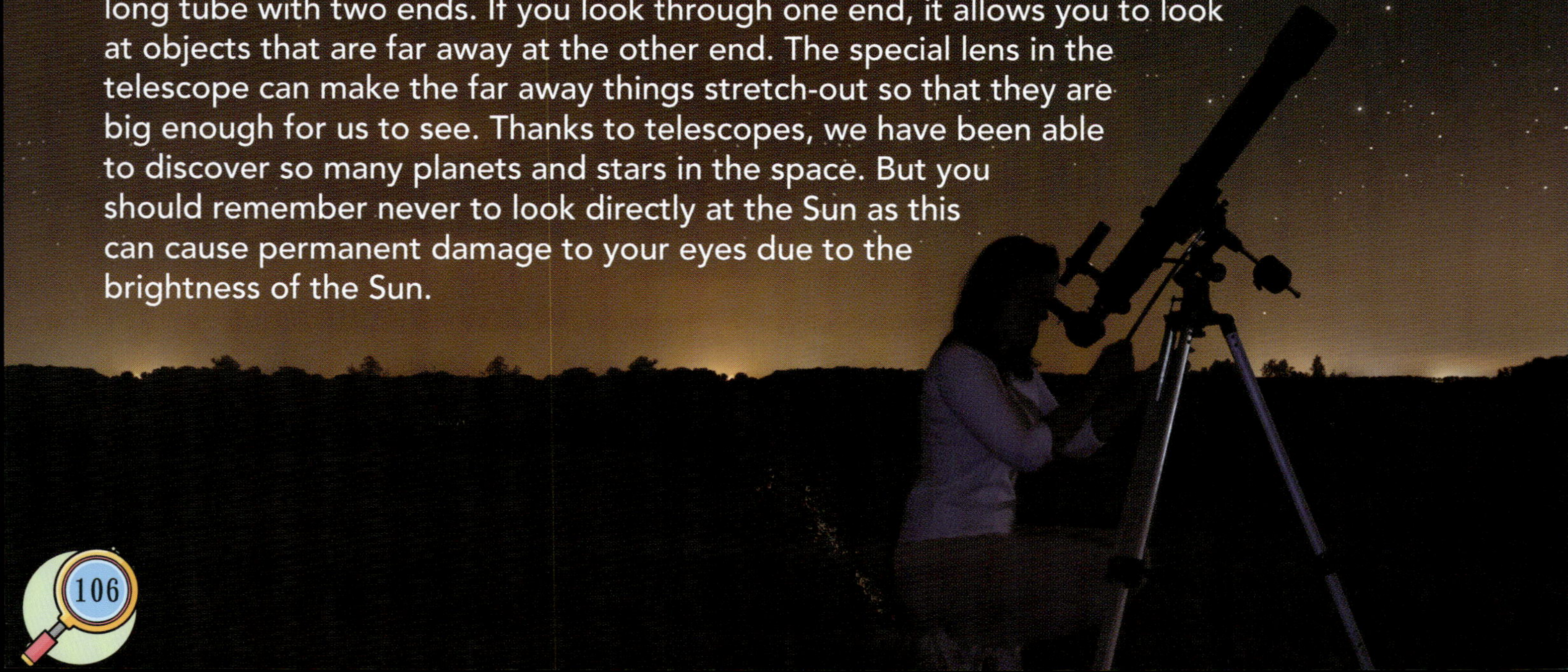

213. Do you know which is the most famous and the most powerful telescope today?

It is the Hubble Space Telescope. It is named after late astronomer Edwin Hubble who proved that the universe is not still but expanding all the time. This huge telescope is not on Earth but floats in space. It was launched into space in 1990 by the space shuttle named Discovery. It takes amazing pictures of objects in space and sends them back to Earth.

Did you know it has been in space since its launch in 1990! It has been serviced and repaired five times since then. Are you wondering if it ever runs out of fuel? It is powered by solar energy through huge solar panels attached to it. The Hubble Space Telescope has been able to take pictures of new galaxies forming in the sky that are otherwise not possible to detect with normal telescopes.

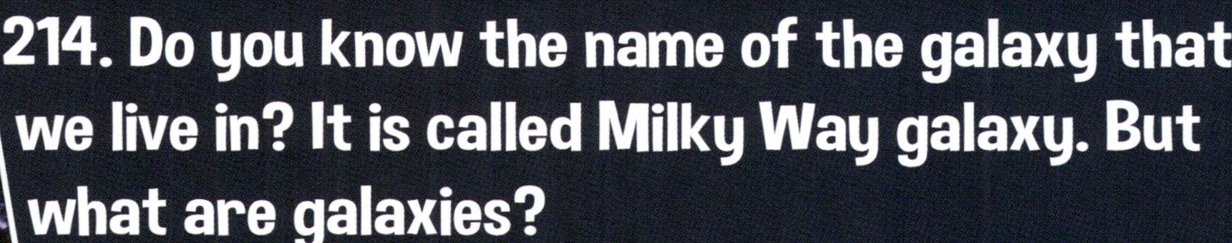

214. Do you know the name of the galaxy that we live in? It is called Milky Way galaxy. But what are galaxies?

Galaxies are huge collections of stars, dust and gas. They usually contain several millions and even more stars of different shapes and brightness. Scientists think there are over 200 billion galaxies in the universe! They are generally separated by large areas of empty space. Galaxies can be spiral, elliptical and even irregular-shaped.

Wow, the universe is so huge! We live in a galaxy called Milky Way. It is a spiral-shaped galaxy that has approximately over 300 billion stars. The Sun is just one of these 300 billion stars and our planet Earth revolves around the Sun.

215. What makes a remote control work? Does it have super powers?

Remote controls are pretty amazing things. With just a press of a button, you can change the volume of the T.V. or turn on the A.C. Have you ever wondered what makes a remote control work?

Ok, let's explore the T.V. remote. If you see carefully, you will find a little spot at the tip of your remote. Does it look like a fake eye or maybe a plastic bead? Yes, you got it right! Have you noticed how this little eye lights up when you press the buttons on your remote? So, when you press the remote buttons, this little eye sends a signal of light to the T.V. Though you cannot see this light but the sensors on T.V. can catch it. So your T.V. now knows what to do.

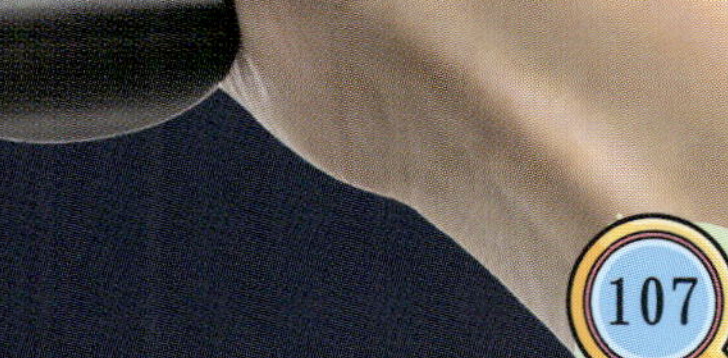

216. How does a refrigerator keep things cold?

You would be surprised to know that the refrigerator keeps things cold because of heat? It's true and let's find out how.

Refrigerant: It is a special liquid inside the refrigerator. It can change from a liquid into gas and again from gas to liquid very fast. The refrigerant absorbs the heat from the food we put in the fridge and evaporates it into gas.

Compressor: It is a pretty cool machine in the refrigerator. It squeezes the gas and pushes it to travel to a coil on the outside of the refrigerator. This gas releases its heat outside of the refrigerator. You can actually feel this heat if you go behind the fridge. On releasing the heat, the gas becomes a liquid again.

Evaporator coils: This liquid passes through a series of evaporator coils inside the refrigerator. These coils change the liquid into cool mist of air. Notice how you feel a cold wave when you open a refrigerator.

The process goes on and on to make the refrigerator work.

217. Why doesn't magnet stick to our hand?

A magnet will not stick to your hand. It only attracts objects that are made of certain metals such as iron and nickel.

What makes a magnet attract iron or nickel objects?

A magnet doesn't have a sticking surface. It has an area around it that has a special force or power. Things, made of iron or nickel, are attracted to this area called a magnetic field.

Let us do a cool experiment to see it. What you need:

A magnet

A sheet of paper Iron shavings (ask your parents to get you this)

Place the magnet under a sheet of paper. Sprinkle iron shavings lightly over the top of the sheet. You will suddenly see the invisible magnetic field as the iron particles stick to it. Do you know how our refrigerator door remains stuck to the fridge? Yes, with a magnet.

218. Do magnets attract other magnets as well?

A magnet has two ends. One end is called the South Pole and another one is called the North Pole. And it doesn't mean these ends have to face north and south directions. These ends can face anyway but they are always at opposite ends of a magnet. So, if you take two bars of magnets and place their north poles together, the magnets will push away from each other. And what do you think will happen if you bring the north pole of one magnet close to the south pole of another magnet? You will hear a clicking sound and the two magnets will stick to each other. This shows that opposite poles attract each other while the same poles repel.

219. Did you know that our Earth is a huge magnet?

The Earth's core is a mix of iron and nickel. This makes the Earth a huge magnet with its unique magnetic field. The Earth too has a North Pole and a South Pole. If you tie a piece of magnet to a wood and let it float in a big bowl of water, the magnet will slowly turn on its own. Its North Pole will point towards the Earth's North Pole. How cool is this? This is how a magnetic compass works. It helps people to find directions when they are lost. What do grownups do today when they are lost while driving? Have you ever heard them talking about using the GPS system on their phone? These systems receive signals from the satellites in the space and tell us where we are. But thousands of years ago when we didn't have smart technology, people relied on magnetic compasses to let them know the directions.

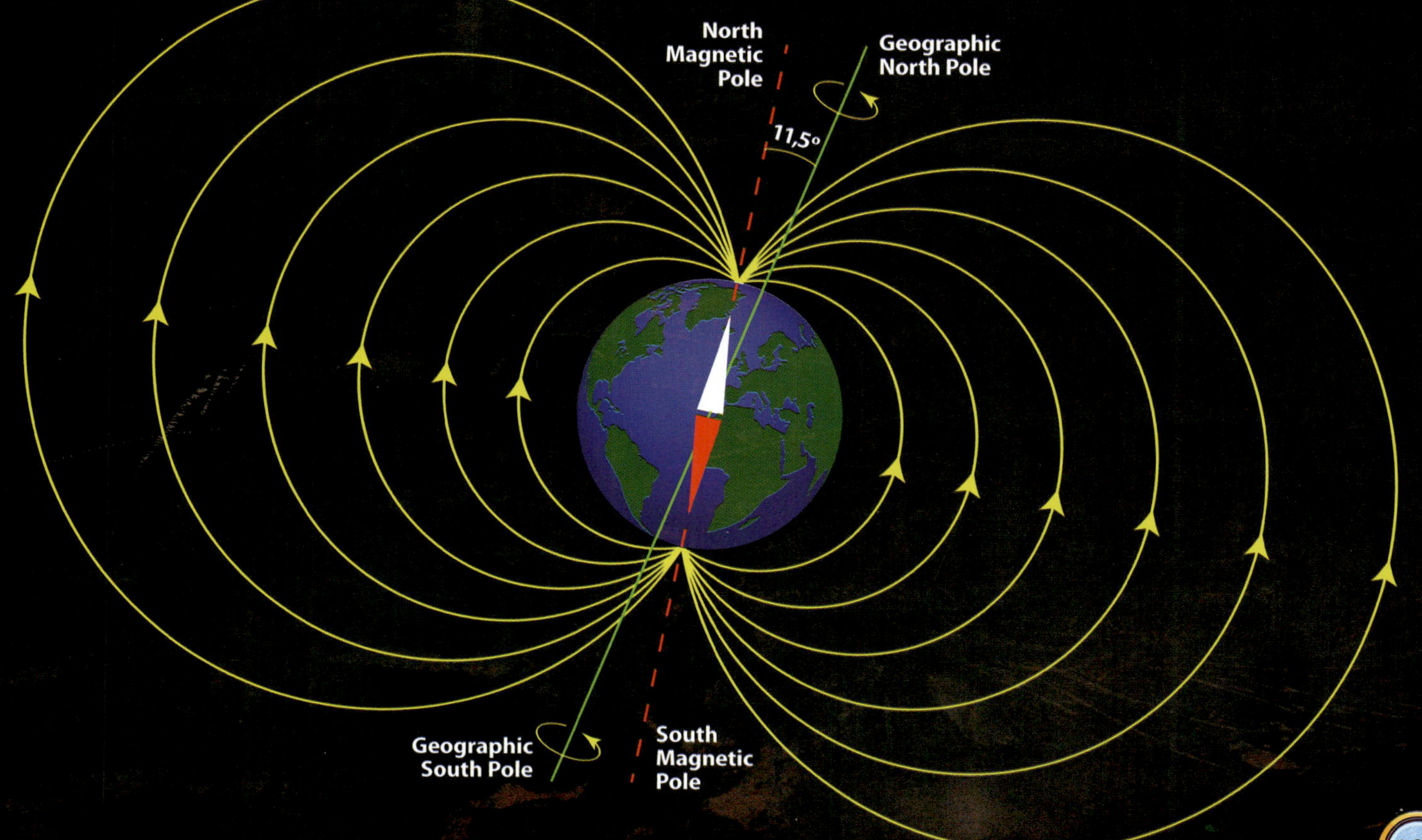

220. Did you know migratory birds never get lost when they migrate long distances?

Scientists believe that birds that need to travel long distances to find warm places for food and shelter are able to find out north and south directions by sensing the earth's magnetic field. They have an in-built magnetic compass it seems! But scientists also think that these birds are very smart. They use the position of Sun as they know it rises in the east and sets in the west. They get an idea of directions from the Sun and other stars. Isn't it amazing how living beings have unique abilities to understand nature in their own ways!

221. Where are the North and South Poles of the Earth?

You may have heard of polar bears and that they live in a very cold place. It is actually the North Pole. And where are penguins found? They also live in cold places where we see blocks of ice all around. Penguins are found on the South Pole. But where are these mysterious places exactly? Let's find out.

Earth spins around on an imaginary line running through it, known as the Earth's axis. The North Pole is present at the northern end of this axis while at the southern axis lies the South Pole. So you can see that both these poles are at opposite ends of the Earth.

222. Who lives on the North Pole?

The North Pole lies in the middle of a frozen Arctic Ocean. Half of the ice melts in summers but freezes again in winters. So it is a difficult and dangerous place to live with shifting ice. No human being actually lives at the North Pole but they live in Arctic regions surrounding it, for example, Russia, Canada, Denmark (Greenland), Norway and the USA (Alaska). But scientists and explorers who need to do a research stay there for some time and come back. So who else lives there? It is home to both land animals such as polar bears, reindeers, foxes and water animals such as walrus, otters, whales, fish, and seals. On the North Pole, the sun rises in March and sets in September. Wow! That's a really long day!

That means Sun is always up during the summer and is always down in winters at the North Pole!

223. Who lives on the South Pole?

South Pole lies in the middle of the Antarctica continent. It is the coldest and driest place on Earth. The South Pole is much cooler than the North Pole. In fact, the temperatures here are so low that snow never melts in some parts of this continent. It is so cold that you cannot stay there for long. Only scientists and their staff live there for some time in special domes just built for these conditions. There are no land animals in Antarctica but it is home to water animals such as blue whale, seals, penguins, fish, krills, squids and birds. Just like at the North Pole, there is 6 months of daylight followed by 6 months of the night at the South Pole. Australia, Fiji, Chile, and Kiribati are some of the countries closest to the South Pole.

224. Is it true that earlier there was only one big land and one big ocean?

Yes. It is true. About 250 million years ago, Earth was one big landmass called Pangaea. It was like a supercontinent. There were changes below the surface of the Earth because of which the land broke down into continents and oceans. The continents then drifted apart. Thus Earth got divided into seven continents-Asia, Africa, North America, South America, Europe, Antarctica and Australia and five oceans -Pacific, Atlantic, Indian, Arctic and Antarctic oceans.

225. Why is the Dead Sea called so?

Imagine a lake with 10 times more salt than an ocean! Can any fish survive in it? No. That is why Dead Sea is called dead. No aquatic animal can survive there.

The Dead Sea is a lake with no outlet. It means that water cannot go out of it. Water from Jordan and its tributaries flow into the Dead Sea bringing with them all sorts of minerals, including salt. Since there is no outlet, the water in the Dead Sea evaporates depositing the dissolved minerals. That is why the Dead Sea has such a high concentration of salt.

Some amazing facts about the Dead Sea-

You can float in the Dead Sea! Yes, this is true. Because of the high salt content, the water becomes dense. This way people become less dense than water and due to buoyancy, they float.

The Dead Sea is also called a 'natural spa'. The minerals and salts found in the lake have the comforting effect, they relax the body and nourish the skin.

You can find 'salt rocks' at the Dead Sea.

The Dead Sea is the lowest point on Earth's surface.

226. Why is ocean water salty?

Water dissolves minerals easily. Salt is one mineral that dissolves very well in water. Now from where does the salt come? Here are the various reasons why oceans have so much salt in its water-

From where does the ocean get water? From lakes and streams. From where do lakes and streams get water? From rain. Rainwater has salt. This water mixes up with lakes and streams that ultimately join the oceans.

The water in lakes and streams passes through soil, rocks and mountains. The soil, rocks and mountains have various minerals including salt. The flowing water keeps absorbing these minerals. This way oceans keep getting a supply of salt.

The amount of salt concentrated in an ocean also depends on how much evaporation takes place. For example - the Dead Sea has the highest level of salt (salinity) because there is no outlet to the sea. No fresh water is being added to it or none leaves. The water keeps evaporating and the salt keeps depositing back.

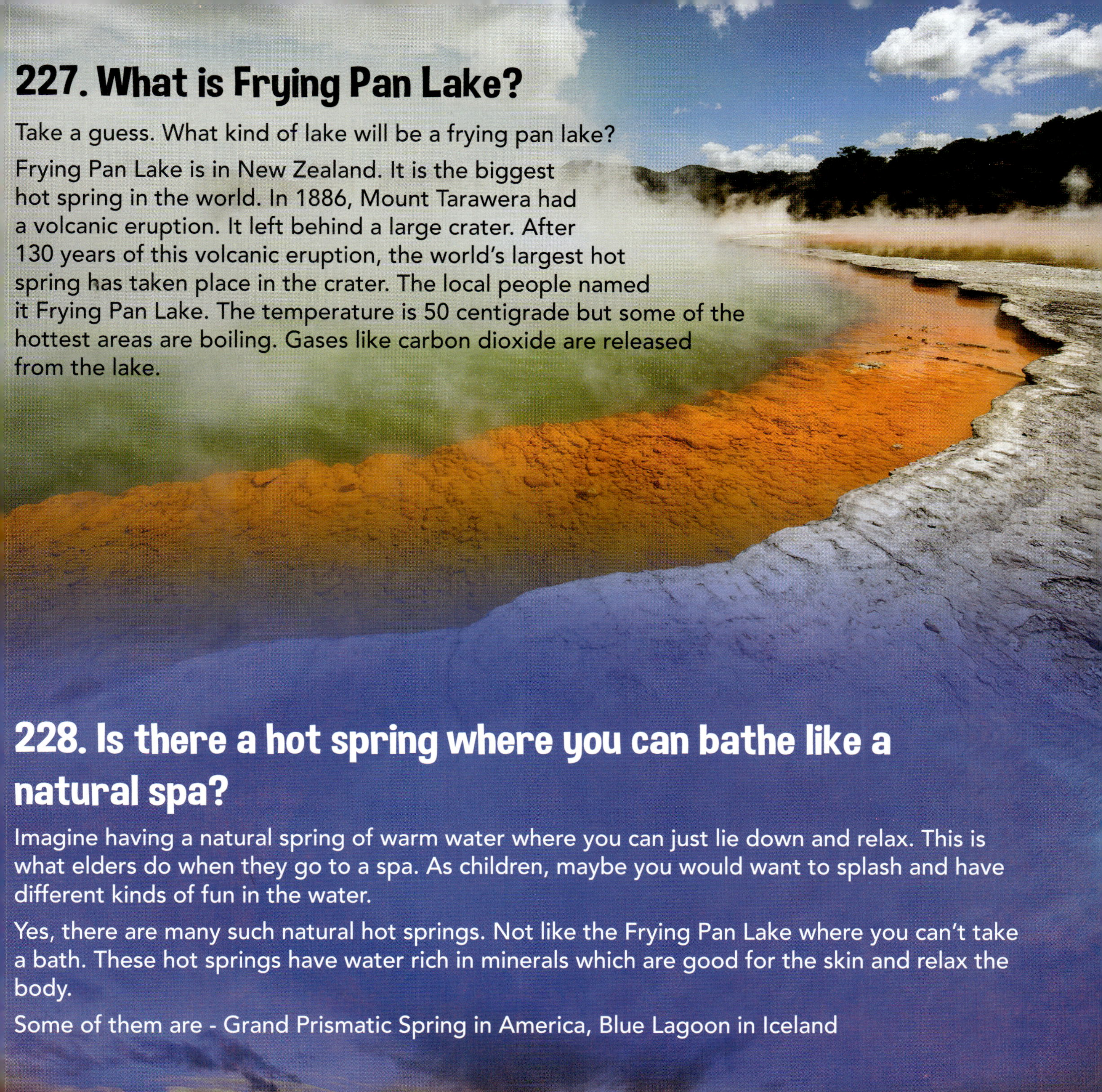

227. What is Frying Pan Lake?

Take a guess. What kind of lake will be a frying pan lake?

Frying Pan Lake is in New Zealand. It is the biggest hot spring in the world. In 1886, Mount Tarawera had a volcanic eruption. It left behind a large crater. After 130 years of this volcanic eruption, the world's largest hot spring has taken place in the crater. The local people named it Frying Pan Lake. The temperature is 50 centigrade but some of the hottest areas are boiling. Gases like carbon dioxide are released from the lake.

228. Is there a hot spring where you can bathe like a natural spa?

Imagine having a natural spring of warm water where you can just lie down and relax. This is what elders do when they go to a spa. As children, maybe you would want to splash and have different kinds of fun in the water.

Yes, there are many such natural hot springs. Not like the Frying Pan Lake where you can't take a bath. These hot springs have water rich in minerals which are good for the skin and relax the body.

Some of them are - Grand Prismatic Spring in America, Blue Lagoon in Iceland

229. Which is the highest waterfall in the world?

Angel Falls in Venezuela is the highest falls. They fall from a height of 979 meters or 3,212 feet. Angel Falls was discovered by an American pilot Jimmy Angels accidentally. He was flying with his wife when his plane crashed at the top of the waterfall. The falls are named after him.

With a height of 979 m (3,212 ft), the falls are located in the Canaima National Park. It is the largest national park in Venezuela and the third largest park in the world. These falls are not fed by melting glaciers, lakes or rivers but by rainfall. During warm seasons, the water of Angel Falls evaporates even before it touches the ground, forming a mist. In the rainy season, Angel Falls become huge again. In fact in the rainy season, the falls separate into two waterfalls. When the water level is high it is possible to feel the water spray up to a mile away.

230. Which is the largest desert?

What comes to mind when you think of a desert? Huge sand dunes and lots of sun? Well, the largest desert is the continent of Antarctica. Almost 98% of the desert is covered with ice. It is sometimes difficult to think of icy Antarctica as a desert, isn't it? But a place is considered a desert if it receives less than 250 millimetres of rainfall or any other form of precipitation annually. Antarctica gets less than 2 inches (50 millimetres) of precipitation a year and that too as snow.

231. Which is the largest hot desert?

The Sahara Desert is the largest hot desert. It is as large as the United States or the entire continent of Europe. But what makes it more interesting is that it is not located in one country. It covers most of the North Africa and more than 8 countries of Africa! The Sahara Desert covers almost 10% of the continent of Africa. It has some of the largest sand dunes in the world. Unlike Antarctica, people live in the Sahara Desert in countries like Egypt, Algeria, Libya, etc. There are animals and plants in it although not many. The highest temperature can be more than 50 centigrade. River Nile provides water to the people living in the desert.

232. Which is the deepest cave known on Earth?

Krubera Cave is the deepest cave on Earth. Imagine climbing inverted Mount Everest. This is how an expedition team described their experience when they explored Krubera Cave. It is located on the edge of the Black Sea in Abkhazia near Georgia. It is 2197 m (7208 feet) deep and is believed to be around the same height as six-and-a-half Eiffel Towers stacked on top of one another. Just like climbing the mountain, the expedition teams move from camp to camp while descending down the cave. There are a lot of limestone, clay and lava rocks inside the cave. The team was surprised to find some transparent fish deep inside the water of the cave, besides meeting the spiders and beetles! What else do you think they could have found out? Imagine and write it down. You may research later and see if some of the things match in your list.

233. Which are the seven natural wonders?

Our planet Earth is full of breathtaking and wonderful sights, all created by Mother Nature. But there are some awe-inspiring creations that are called the '7 Natural Wonders'. They are:

The Great Barrier Reef

Mount Everest

Grand Canyon

The Harbor at Rio de Janeiro

Victoria Falls

Parícutin

Northern Lights

234. Where is the Great Barrier Reef?

Imagine 400 types of coral reefs spread over 3000 km. Imagine hundreds of variety of fish in all kinds of colours floating around. That is the Great Barrier Reef.

The Great Barrier Reef is the largest coral reef system in the world. It is located in Australia. And you know what, the Great Barrier Reef is so huge that it can be seen from the space as well!

It is the most fascinating reef where you can spot hundreds of varieties of fish, sea turtles, dolphins, even whales! It is also the only home for the two endangered animals - the green sea turtle and dugong (sea cow).

235. What is so special about Mount Everest?

Mount Everest is the highest mountain in the world. It is 29,035 feet or 8848 metres tall. This is around the height, passenger airplanes fly! It means that it is as tall as 20 Empire State Buildings stacked on top of each other! It lies in the Himalayas between Nepal and Tibet. It is covered with snow all year round. It can get as cold as -80 F on Mount Everest! Water freezes at 32 F. So imagine how cold it will be on Mount Everest!

Climbing this peak is the dream of most of the mountaineers. Sir Edmund Hillary and Tenzing Norgay were the first to climb this amazing peak in 1953. 13-year-old Jordan Romero is the youngest person to climb it. So far around 4000 people have tried to climb Mt. Everest. It takes approximately 40 days to climb the mountain. There are 18 different routes to climb.

In 2010, Burj Khalifa in Dubai became the world's tallest building and the tallest man-made structure of any kind but Everest is more than ten times its height.

236. What is the Grand Canyon?

Surrounded by cliffs, the Grand Canyon is like a deep valley. It is 6000 feet deep! It is so wide and so deep that it can be seen from the space! It is located in Arizona, USA.

It got created when water from River Colorado carried away a huge amount of soil from this place. Over the years, a deep valley was created there. Many animals and birds live in Grand Canyon. Some tribal people still live there. The rocks found in the Grand Canyon are millions of years old. These rocks are very important for research.

The Grand Canyon was converted into a National Park in 1919. That means you can take a vacation and explore this amazing creation of nature. You can trek, hike and camp as you explore its spectacular beauty!

237. Is the Harbor at Rio de Janeiro really spectacular?

Rio De Janeiro is called the marvellous city and it is called so mainly because of the spectacular Harbour. The Portuguese sailors discovered Brazil in 1501. As they moved, they felt their ships were entering a river. But it turned out to be a bay surrounded by mountains. (Bay is a water body surrounded by land on 3 sides.) Since they had come in January, they named the harbour Rio De Janeiro meaning January River.

This Bay is called the Guanabara bay which is 32 km long and is surrounded by mountains. Just at the entrance of the bay, stands a lopsided mountain which is 1299 feet tall. It is made of granite and an amazing sight. You can explore this mountain on a cable car ride. Then there is the statue of 'Christ the Redeemer' that adds to its beauty. The bay has several beaches that stretch over a distance of 80 km. As many as 130 islands adorn the bay. The city itself has settled around the harbour. It must be seen to be believed!

238. Why are Victoria Falls considered one of the natural wonders?

Victoria Falls may not be the widest or the highest but they have the maximum volume of water that falls. That makes them the most amazing waterfall in the world. They are twice wider and twice higher than the Niagara Falls in America. They are located on the border of Zambia and Zimbabwe. Let's see why they are one of the seven wonders of nature-

Moonbow - On a full moon night, you can see a moonbow on the Victoria Falls! This is visible during the night in the spray of water.

Two national parks surround and protect the Victoria Falls. They make the falls a very beautiful place. The forests are full of zebras, hippopotamus, rhinoceros, giraffe, etc.

A bridge has been made on the falls which is the highest bridge in the world.

239. What is Parícutin?

Parícutin is the name of the volcano that erupted in a small village of Mexico from 1943 to 1952. It was the first volcano that the scientists could observe right from its eruption (active) till it became dormant (dead) in 1952.

Pulido was a farmer who was working in a village just outside Parícutin. He was the first person to notice the volcano. In a cornfield, there was a small hill. He noticed grey ashes coming out of the crack of the hill and then lava erupting. The volcano remained active during the first year of the eruption. Then it slowed down till it finally went dormant in 1952. Due to large deposits of lava and volcano sands, the village had to be emptied. The volcano stands 1345 feet above the ground. Nearly 1000 people died during its eruptions. Volcanoes surely are very dangerous!

240. What makes Northern Lights a natural wonder?

Imagine the sky lit with various colours in so many patterns! First green, then pink, red, orange and then turning into violet! All changing one after the other on their own!

The Northern Lights, also known as auroras, are lights that naturally occur in the sky. They create amazing displays in the sky and appear in different patterns. They fall like curtains, shine like rays and even bounce like waves across the sky. It seems as if the lights are dancing. They appear in all kinds of colours red, orange, violet but the most common is pink and pale green. The colours may keep changing on their own or remain the same for hours.

The Northern Lights are produced when the electrically charged particles from the sun enter the atmosphere of the Earth. Some of the places where you can see the Northern lights are some north-west regions of Canada and the southern tip of Greenland and Iceland.

241. Just like natural wonders, do you know there are seven man-made wonders of the world?

Just like some Natural Wonders leave you spellbound, man has also created monuments, buildings and cities that amaze everyone. There is a foundation called 'The New seven wonders Foundation' which has declared seven wonders of the world. Twenty-one monuments were shortlisted and then voted by the people of the world. Egyptians were not happy that The Great Pyramid of Giza will have to compete with modern buildings. So that is why it is considered an honorary candidate.

Petra

Great Wall of China

Taj Mahal

Machu Picchu

Chichén Itzá

Colosseum

Christ the Redeemer

The Great Pyramid of Giza (honorary candidate)

242. How do you pronounce Chichén Itzá and what is it ?

Roll your tongue and lips and say *chee-chehn eet-sah!* Easy? Keep trying and you will get it very soon. It is not just the name of the city but the city itself that is unique. *Chichen* means at the mouth of the well of *Itza*. It is an ancient city in Mexico that was built during Maya Civilisation. The city has been built in a way that it speaks of every detail of how the Maya Civilisation established and then progressed each year. The 4 sides of Chichén Itza contain 365 steps (depicting the solar year), 52 panels (for each year in the Mayan century as well as each week in the solar year) and 18 terraces (for the 18 months in the religious year). There is an observatory in Chichén Itzá which is called Caracol. This shows the scientific and astronomical achievements of the Mayans. Their astronomical skills were so advanced that they could even predict solar eclipses. There are impressive monuments and buildings in the city, all of them are built out of stone. The most recognisable structure is the Temple of Kukulkan also known as El Castillo. If you clap your hand in the temple, it echoes back the same sound as the chirping of the Quetzal bird. The Quetzal bird is the sacred bird associated with God Kulkulkan. Amazing, isn't it?

243. What is Christ the Redeemer?

Christ the Redeemer is a statue in Rio de Janeiro, Brazil. When you look at the statue, it seems that Jesus Christ is welcoming all the people with a hug! This statue of Jesus is one of Rio de Janeiro's most widely recognised monuments. It stands 98 feet tall on the summit of Mount Corcovado. The mount itself is more than 2,300 feet high and the statue weighs approximately 700 tons. To see the statue closely, you can ride a steam engine train up the steep 2.3-mile slope. If you ever visit the statue, rest up on the ride because at the rail's end you have more than 200 steps to climb to get to the foot of the statue!

244. Where is the Colosseum?

The Colosseum is in Italy. Built-in Rome sometime around AD 70, it was the first and largest freestanding amphitheatre. The Colosseum has 80 entrances and can accommodate an audience of nearly 50,000 people! The Colosseum was used for gladiator contests where men fought other men or wild animals. These events used to sometime go on for 100 days at a stretch! Around 60,000 Jewish slaves took 9 years to build this magnificent building.

The Colosseum has been renovated many times but still, weather and natural disasters have left their impact on it. Visitors flock to this amazing sight daily! If you wish to see it, you can watch the movie 'Gladiator'. Well, you can see a version of it with special effects.

245. What is so special about the Taj Mahal?

The Taj Mahal is the most magnificent symbol of love. Shah Jahan, the fifth Mughal (or Mogul) Emperor built it as a memorial to his deceased wife Mumtaz Mahal, who died during childbirth. He was so pained by her death that he built the Taj Mahal as a place that would remain like a beautiful memory. Many people from all over the world dream to marry at the Taj Mahal as it stands as a symbol of love.

The Taj Mahal is located in Agra. It is made of white marble which was brought from various countries like Afghanistan, China and Arabia. Its construction took more than two decades (20 years). It required more than 20,000 labourers and cost several million rupees. Various passages from the Quran (the holy book of Islam) are inscribed in the walls of the structure. Many precious and semi-precious stones have been used to enhance the beauty of this one of its kind monument. It is a stunning and well-known Indian landmark.

246. What is so great about The Great Wall of China?

The Great Wall of China is the longest structure ever built by man. The wall is 8,851 kilometres long! It is 25 feet tall and 15-30 feet wide (almost wide enough for two cars to pass). Records show that more than 300,000 soldiers and 500,000 people worked to build it.

It was built over more than 2000 years ago. The construction began in the 7th Century BC by the ruling powers to keep the enemy from invading the place. The first Emperor of China, Qin Shihuang started to build it further to protect his northern borders. Though he started it but construction of the wall continued with the later kings and dynasties. Most of the Great Wall that we see today was built in the Ming Dynasty (1368-1644). It is a myth that the structure is a single continuous wall. In fact, it is a collection of short walls, with thousands of lookout towers that extend through plains, grasslands and even mountains!

247. What is so special about Petra?

Petra is a city in Jordan which has been carved out of rocks! Petra means rock in Greek and that is why it is also known as 'the city in the rock'. It is located in a desert valley surrounded by cliffs of sandstone. The Arabs who settled some 2000 years ago carved the cliffs to create temples, gateways, tombs, theatres, halls, streets and monuments. There are about 800 carved tombs in Petra. Right in the middle of the desert, the Arabs established a very efficient water system for Petra. Because of the colour, it is also known as the red rose city. Early morning or late afternoon, when the sun warms the stones, the city looks majestic.

248. What is Machu Picchu?

Machu Picchu is a city in Peru. Machu Picchu means 'Old mountain'. If Petra is the city in the rock, then Machu Picchu is the city in the clouds. Built in the 15th century, the city is located 8,000 feet above sea level, atop a mountain in the Andes Mountains. The three sides of the city are surrounded by cliffs and the fourth side by a high mountain. The entire city has been built of stone and they say no wheel was used to transport the stones! The stones of the buildings are stuck together without mortar (cement like thing used to join two things). The stones in the buildings are cut so precisely that not even a credit card can be inserted between them. Interestingly, the city falls in the line of earthquake. So whenever an earthquake strikes, the stones 'dance' and fall in their original place after the tremors subside. And no buildings fall! There are some 140 buildings in the city.

249. What is a MUMMY?

The most common known meaning of Mummy is that they are dead bodies preserved by the Egyptians. But a Mummy can be a dead body of any person whose fleshy parts have been preserved.

The Egyptians believed that they should preserve the soul of the man who has died. It was believed that this will help them have a great 'after life' (life after death). That is why they would remove some of the organs, apply preservatives to dry the body and wrap the body in a linen cloth to preserve the dead body. Gradually, this became a status symbol for the wealthy and better methods of embalming (putting preservatives and balms) were invented.

Is the thought of a Mummy scary? Well, it can be. Mummy has been used as a character to create a series of movies namely 'The Mummy' and 'The Mummy Returns'.

250. Can a dead body get automatically converted into a Mummy?

Let's first try to understand why a dead body needs to be preserved. When a person or an animal dies, bacteria on the body cause it to decompose. What is left behind eventually is just the skeleton. So, if the conditions are such that the bacteria cannot grow, a body will be mummified or preserved!

Therefore, dead bodies are mummified sometimes accidentally by nature. In 1984, scientists discovered the mummies of three English sailors in the Canadian Arctic (where it is extremely cold). These bodies were in such good shape that one of the scientists remarked that they looked like they were still alive, just unconscious. But these sailors had been dead for about 150 years!

251. Which is the oldest Mummy found so far?

'The Ice Man', in the body of Ötzi is the oldest well-preserved human mummy in the world. Can you guess how old is it? About 5,300 years!

Hikers found 'The Ice Man', in the body of Ötzi frozen in a glacier in the Alps near the border of Italy and Austria. By studying his body and the clothing and tools that were found with him, scientists are trying to figure out who the Ice Man was and how he lived and died.

252. What is a volcano?

A volcano is a mountain which has molten rocks beneath the surface of the earth. When there is a crack in the earth's surface, the molten rock erupts out of the mountain. The molten rock is called lava.

The hot lava flows and causes destruction all around. Volcanoes can cause floods, earthquakes and tsunamis. The lava may eventually cool down to form mountains and even fertile soil. A rough estimate says that there are 1500 volcanoes out of which 80 are under the oceans. Over half of the volcanoes are located in the Pacific Ocean in an arc called the 'Ring of Fire'.

253. What is a hurricane?

Hurricanes are huge storms. When strong winds blow over the ocean surface, they take energy and heat from the warm ocean waters and become a hurricane. If the wind is not strong or the heat is not enough, the hurricane is not formed.

Hurricanes are like huge engines that convert the warmth of the oceans into large winds and waves. They can extend upto 400 miles. The centre of a hurricane is called an 'eye'. It is calm at the eye but major danger lies in the area around the eye called the 'eyewall'. A hurricane lasts for a week and keeps moving at a speed of 10-20 miles per hour on the ocean surface. When the hurricane reaches the shore, it can cause massive destruction with its winds and rains killing millions of people.

254. Why are hurricanes named after women like Hurricane Katrina, Hurricane Lisa, Hurricane Sandy?

Naming of cyclones by the name of people began in 1945. Giving names made it easier to track and describe a particular cyclone. Earlier names of saints and politicians were used. Hurricanes or cyclones are named not only after women. Alternate male and female name is given to cyclones. So if you will look up in the internet, you will find hurricane Barry, Hurricane Andrew and so on.

255. In the movie 'The Impossible', there was a big tsunami. What is a tsunami?

A tsunami is a series of ocean waves that take place due to an earthquake, a landslide or a volcanic eruption in the ocean. The first wave may not be strong. But the rest of the waves become stronger and bigger. The waves can rise up to 100 feet and can travel as fast as jet planes.

In 2004, a tsunami in the Indian Ocean killed about 230,000–280,000 people! 11 countries right from East Africa to Thailand were affected by the killer waves of the tsunami. It happened due to an earthquake in the Indian Ocean. It is believed that it had the energy of as many as 23,000 atomic bombs! The movie 'The Impossible' is based on the tsunami of 2004. It is inspired by a true story!

256. Why do earthquakes happen?

Imagine holding a cane. Put pressure on both the ends of the cane. After some time, the cane will bend and then break. This is the way a cane deals with the stress that you have put on it. The Earth deals with stress in a similar way. The inner layers of the Earth are made of plates. When these plates stretch or squeeze, they put pressure on each other. When the pressure is large enough, the huge rocks in the Earth shift and Earth's crust breaks. This causes the Earth to shake and an earthquake happens.

257. Can we measure earthquakes?

The magnitude of the earthquake is measured on the Richter Scale. Charles F. Richter had invented the Richter Scale in 1935. According to it, if the earthquake measures 5, then it will shake the ground 10 times more than an earthquake that measures 4.

The Sumatra-Andaman earthquake that hit on 26th December, 2004 is the longest earthquake to have ever hit Earth. A small earthquake lasts for a second and mid-size earthquake for a few seconds but this earthquake lasted for 500-600 seconds which is full 10 minutes! It measured between 9.1-9.3 and had the power of 100 gigantic bombs. It also caused the largest gush in the sea bed. It hit the Indian Ocean and caused the deadly tsunami. This earthquake shook Planet Earth!

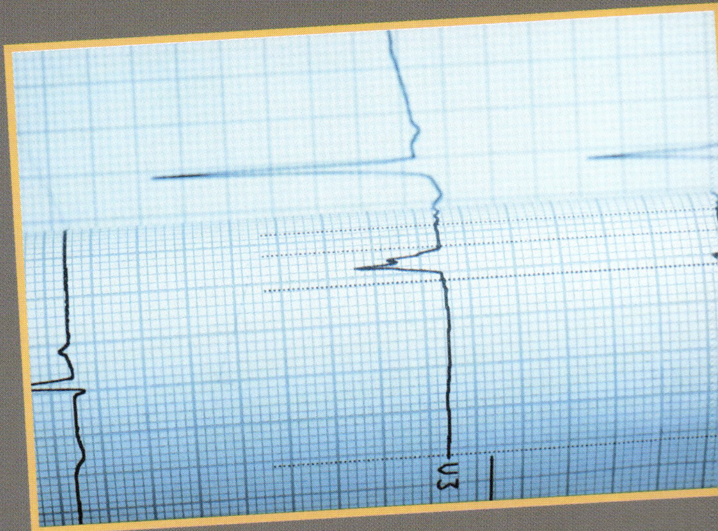

258. How are discoveries made?

Explorers and discoverers are people who are constantly questioning. When they question, they try to find. That is how new discoveries and inventions are made.

That is why we use the word 'known'. Till the time some new discovery is not made, that thing holds the record. But remember, records are made to be broken! But there is a difference between discoveries and inventions. You can only discover something that already exists. But you invent something that doesn't exist before or has not been created before!

259. Who invented the mobile phone?

Like many other inventions, the mobile phone is the product of hard work and research of many inventors.

It was as early as 1900 when an inventor named Reginald Fessenden made his first wireless call. He was the first one to transmit human voice using radio waves, using a signal from one radio tower to another.

In 1947, an engineer named William Young along with another engineer D. H. Ring started work on how a person can move around from one radio tower to another and still be on the call. It took 10 years before this become a reality.

Richard H. Frenkiel and Joel S. Engel were successful in building a network that could support moving around with a cell phone. But there were issues.

Finally, in 1973, Martin Cooper came out with the first commercial cell phone. It was heavy and big like a brick. But improvements were rapid. Today, we have sleek mobile phones which can be connected almost anywhere.

260. Why should we switch off our mobile phones when the flight is about to take off?

Mobile phones release electromagnetic waves. The safety systems and other equipment in the aircraft also operate on the basis of a certain frequency of waves. The problem can arise if the mobiles transmit waves of the same frequency as the equipment. It can send wrong signals or no signals, confusing the pilots.

Switching off mobiles is a preventive step. It has not been proved so far that mobiles create problems in the equipment and system of the aeroplane. But as a precaution, crew in the aeroplanes asks the passengers to switch off mobiles at the time when the aircraft is about to fly or land. After reaching a certain height, the chances of frequency getting mixed is less. But many aeroplanes don't allow using mobiles at all on the flight.

261. How do mobile phones work?

A mobile phone or a cell phone works by sending signals through the air. There are special towers build on the roads that catch these signals and send these to the person you are calling from your cell. The microphone in the cell phone converts these signals into sound and your voice will be heard!

262. How does a landline telephone work?

A telephone is different than a cell phone. Unlike a cell phone, the telephone is connected to a wire at one end. It also sends signals like a cell phone does. But it sends signals through wires instead of air. These wires are laid under the ground and carry these signals to the person you are calling. The microphone in the phone converts these signals into sound.

263. Who invented zero?

Some children love Math while some don't like it much. Well, you may like Math or not but can you imagine Math without the number zero? The entire Math is impossible without the number zero. And you will not have any computers today if zero was not there!

So who was the genius who invented math? Aryabhatta, an Indian astronomer and mathematician, invented zero. Before he invented zero, it was just used as a symbol for 'empty', 'nothing', 'space'. He gave place value and used zero in equations.

264. Who was the first to discover that Earth is not flat but a sphere (round)?

People earlier believed that Earth was flat. But they were confused as no explorer had seen the edge of Earth. They could not explain the logic behind the following facts:

Where do the tides of the sea go when they reach the end of the Earth?

Why don't the ships fall when they reach the edge?

It was Plato who first suggested that Earth could be a sphere and not flat. He said there was no end but a round circumference that was continuous.

It was a Portuguese explorer named Ferdinand Magellan who proved that Earth was round. In 1519, he took a voyage which lasted for 3 years and went all round the Earth (circumnavigate) to prove that Earth was round and not flat!

265. But wait, you thought that the Earth is a perfect sphere?

Think again. The glaciers at the North and the South Poles are very heavy and put extreme pressure on the land beneath them. The Antarctic ice cap is so heavy that it compresses the earth slightly at the South Pole, making it slightly pear-shaped. It was Sir Isaac Newton who first proposed that Earth was not perfectly round. He suggested that it is little squashed at its poles and swollen at the equator.

266. Who discovered that Earth is not at the centre of the Universe?

For centuries it was believed that the Earth was the center of the universe. In 1543, a man named Copernicus published a book asking 'What if the Earth was a planet circling the Sun?' He didn't actually prove but claimed that the Sun, not the Earth, was the center of the universe, and that many planets revolved around the Sun. His book was banned by the Church. Later, an astronomer Galileo Galilei proved Copernicus' theory. He looked at the universe through his first telescope and found:

He discovered that four moons circled around Jupiter which meant that everything did not revolve around Earth, as believed earlier.

He also observed that Venus went in phases just like Moon which proved that it didn't orbit around Earth but around Sun.

His discoveries were questioned by the Church and he was imprisoned for telling lies!

267. Who was Christopher Columbus?

Christopher Columbus was a courageous sailor and a discoverer. He was born in 1451 in Italy. It was a very exciting time as people were busy discovering new things and places. Christopher too learnt how to make maps and navigate a ship. During his time, people from Europe travelled east to China and East Asia to do business. But all the known routes were either too dangerous or too long. He proposed finding a new route by sailing west on the Atlantic Ocean. He thought that as Earth is round, he would reach East Asia faster.

For seven years Christopher travelled around Europe looking for someone who would finance his journey. Finally, the king and queen of Spain agreed to support him. With three ships, he set sail. What he didn't realise was that there was another land between Europe and Asia. It was America. When finally he reached the island of Bahamas in 1459, he thought that he was in India. He named the island San Salvador.

268. Who invented the television?

A young boy named Philo Taylor Farnsworth invented what we call television. Can you imagine your life without T.V.? All those cartoons, movies, songs and entertainment we can watch today because of Philo.

Philo loved to see trains come and go. People who invented the telegraph and other machines were his heroes. He used to live in a log cabin but then his family moved into a new city. There he lived in a proper house with wires. He was fascinated by all the wiring and electricity. He had this big idea when he was just 13 how an electric beam can be used to scan pictures and display on the screen. But it took him many years to finally create a model of T.V. So, thanks to Philo that you can have some real fun with T.V.

269. Who invented the telephone?

Alexander Graham Bell was the first person to invent a model with which voice messages could be sent. He was born in Scotland. Graham Bell had been trying to use electricity to send telegraphic messages for a long time. Due to a lack of time and equipment, he took the help of Thomas Watson in a nearby electrical shop. They became good friends. It was on 2nd June 1875 that Graham heard a message over the wire from Watson who was working in the next room. But the instrument could only transmit voice sound and not words. He worked hard on the device and finally in 1876, a sentence could be heard over the phone! He then finally declared his invention to the entire world!

270. What did scientists do when Albert Einstein died?

When Albert Einstein died, it is said that Dr. Harvey at Princeton Hospital convinced his son to keep his brain for research. All the world wanted to find out what made Einstein such a genius! The Research said that the part of the brain that takes care of speech and language was small in Einstein's case while the part that takes care of numbers was much larger. But no one is sure if the research was right and no one really knows what made Einstein so intelligent!

Albert Einstein was someone who always questioned what he was told. Because of his questioning, he researched on many theories. And what did he find? He found new laws and theories on which modern physics and mathematics is based. Einstein believed in imagination. He started building models at a very young age. He has said, 'Imagination is more powerful than knowledge'. His most important contribution has been the 'Theory of Relativity'. This theory helped scientists in understanding the Sun and the planets.

271. How many times did Thomas Edison fail before he invented the bulb?

It is said that Thomas Edison failed more than 9000 times in inventing the bulb! A young reporter asked him once, 'Do you consider yourself a failure?' Edison replied, 'Not at all. I now know 9000 ways how the bulb cannot be invented'. They say finally after that, Edison was successful in inventing the bulb. Can you imagine your life without a bulb?

272. When was the first bus invented?

Can you imagine how the first bus might have looked like? In 1662, a man named Blaise Pascal took a carriage with several seats and horses and launched the first bus service in Paris. It was meant for the rich and famous people in the society but after 15 years the service was stopped. Then in 1824, a man named Greenwood repeated the same thing. The service extended to various cities from Paris and it was successful.

It was in 1830, that Walter Hancock and Sir Goldsworthy Gurney invented the steam carriage. Every passing year, the model of the bus kept changing till we got modern buses. From single decker to double decker, today buses have some of the most modern look and facilities.

273. When was the first train invented?

In 1813, George Stephenson began working on the first train. He was only 20 years old at that time. Everything in those times was handmade. So, a blacksmith assisted George in hammering and making the engine and the train. It took ten months of hard work to build the train and it was tested on a track in 1814. It was the first successful train.

George Stephenson went on to make 16 different engines. He built the first public railway: the Stockton and Darlington railway in 1825. Stephenson was the chief engineer for several of the railways.

274. How did James Watt invent the steam engine?

When James Watt was a little boy, he saw how the steam escapes from the tea kettle. He was fascinated by steam from then. He was curious to know how steam had the power to lift the lid!

When Watt was working in a shop, a steam pump model was brought for repair. He observed the pump and realised how the cylinder was heated and then cooled down. This let to wastage of power. He realised the cylinder has to be kept hot, like at the time when the steam entered it. This led him to experiment for many months. Finally, in 1765, at the age of 29, James Watt saw that his idea worked.

James Watt had the idea and understanding but could not practically produce the steam engine. It took 11 years before he could see his invention become reality. He took help of an industrialist John Roebuck to give a practical shape to the steam engine.

275. Who invented the car?

There are many inventors who contributed to what we today know as a car. They improved and developed the model every year.

Leonardo Da Vinci had made the sketch of the first car.

In 1769, Nicholas Joseph Cugnot made the steam engine that moved on its own.

Robert Anderson made the first electronic carriage but it needed to be charged again and again.

Gottlieb Daimler made the first gasoline engine.

The overall credit goes to Karl Benz. In 1886, it was he who invented a car that resembled the modern car, was successful and ran on gasoline. By 1888, he had produced 3 models of cars in private. After he joined hands with Dailmer Company, he died.

276. What was Henry Ford's contribution to the modern cars?

Henry Ford did not invent the car but he gave a future to the car industry. His leadership ability and grand vision encouraged car makers that this industry could be so huge and successful.

Henry Ford grew up on a farm but machines attracted him. He used to open and then put back people's watches. He got limited education but his curiosity to find out led to do various things. At the age of 15, he made his own steam engine. He made a horseless carriage called quadricycle.

Henry joined the Detroit Automobile Company and as the chief engineer, made several cars. Then he opened his own company and started making racing cars. He was successful and attracted bankers to invest in his experiments. In 1903, he founded his company called Ford Motor Company. Then there was no looking back. Henry Ford introduced the concept of making cars on a mass scale (large number). He changed the face of the automobile industry.

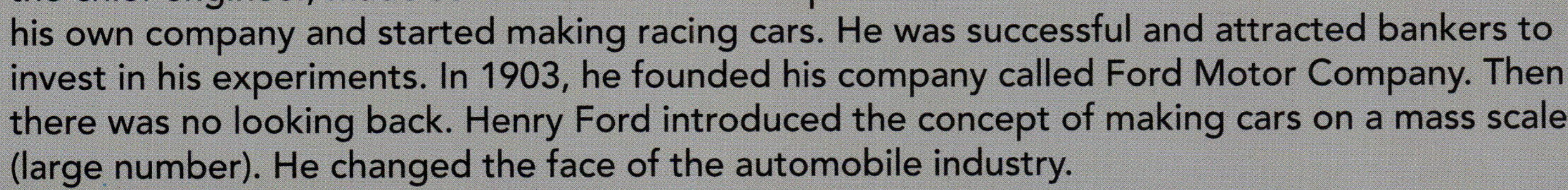

Today, you see such a large variety of cars being produced in so many countries in so many numbers. It is because one man named Henry Ford started it all.

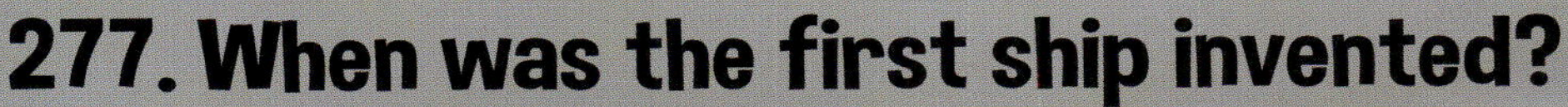

277. When was the first ship invented?

The first-ever ship was invented by the Egyptians. They sailed boats in the River Nile. By 2500 BC, they started making wooden boats. Over the years, the ships and the boats were improved. In 1819, the first ship to be run on steam and wind power was built. In 1845, the first ship of iron was made. With time, instead of coal, ships began to use diesel as fuel.

In 1959, a cargo ship named Savannah (that carries goods) was built that used nuclear power as fuel. It could run for 3 and a half years without refuelling! Today, there are cargo ships that can carry a thousand containers. There are ships called cruise liners on which people holiday for many days.

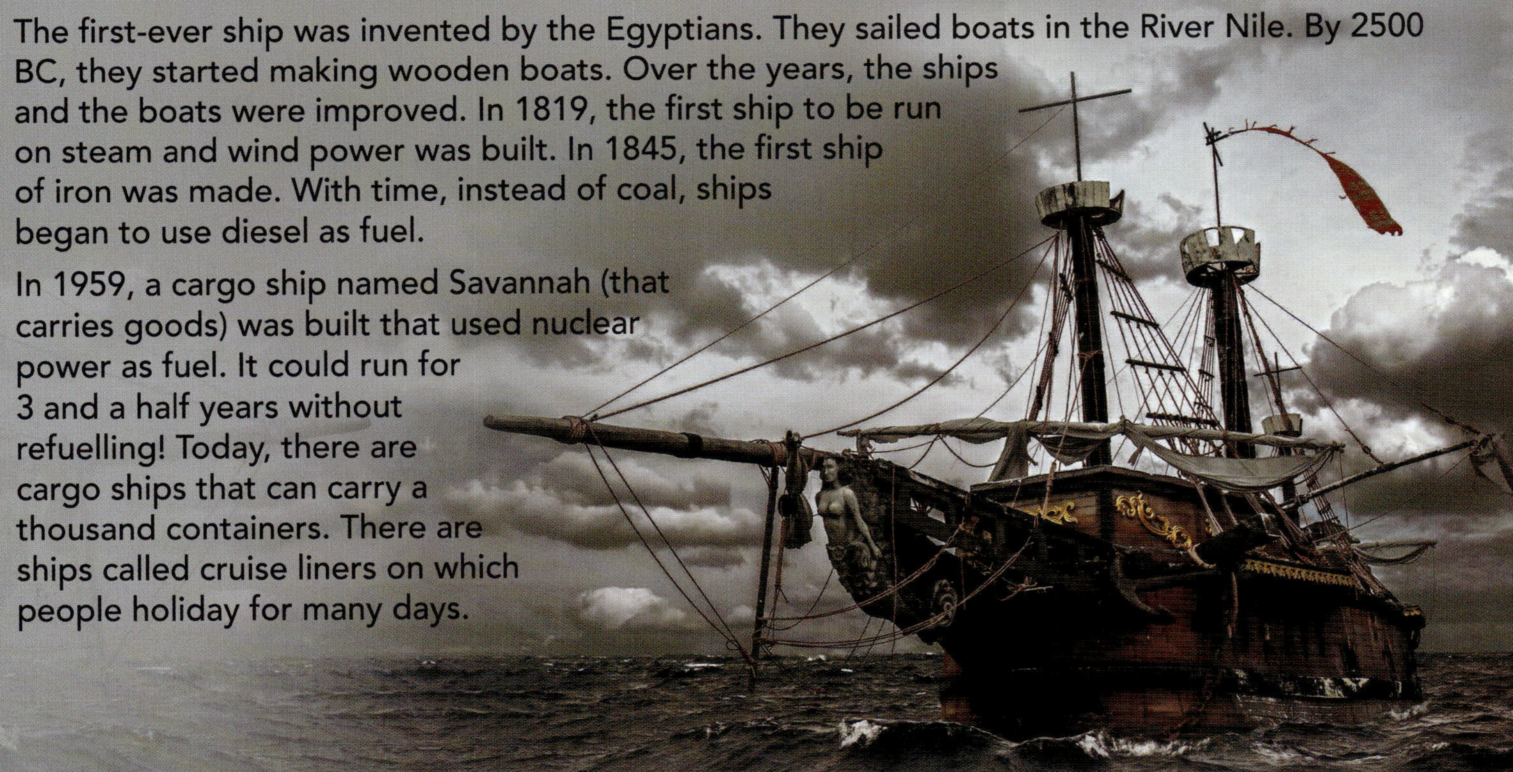

278. Was there really a ship named Titanic that sank?

It is said that it was a no moon night on 14th April. That is why the iceberg that hit Titanic could not be seen. The temperature of the ocean was -2 centigrade. The total number of people on the ship was 2223, out of which more than 1500 people died.

279. Who invented the aeroplane?

Orville and Wilbur Wright were two brothers who had first invented the aeroplane. The first successful flight took place in 1903. The first aeroplane was made of wood and it flew for 12 seconds.

There were many people before Wright Brothers who tried to invent an aeroplane. But it was these two brothers who were successful in taking the plane forward, up and down. The Wright Brothers made several attempts in 1901 and 1902 but were not successful. It was in 1903 that the first plane flew. Then there was no looking back. In 1904, they created a new model and the flight lasted for one and a half minute. In 1905, the plane flew for 33 minutes 17 seconds. It took many more years to refine this model and finally, we had the modern aeroplanes. Now you can fly for hours in the air, sitting comfortably watching movies and sipping your favourite juice, thanks to Wright Brothers!

280. What is dynamite?

Dynamite is an explosive made by mixing many chemicals. These chemicals burst with lots of pressure and heat. So, an explosive can be very dangerous as it can destroy everything that is present around it. Dynamite was used in wars. But now it is mainly used in quarrying and mining. Here, huge blocks of rocks or small hills are blown. It is done to extract minerals and metals that are inside the earth. It is also used in construction and demolition where a building or a structure is blown away to create flat grounds or to make passages for roads and dams. Before dynamite got its name, it was called 'Nobel's blasting powder' as it was invented by Alfred Nobel.

281. What is a Nobel Prize?

Nobel Prize is the most prestigious prize awarded to people who make outstanding and special contribution in the field of physics, chemistry, economics, literature, peace and medicine. The person gets a gold medal, a sum of money (in 2012 it was 1.2 million U.S dollars!) and a diploma.

The award is named after Swedish inventor Alfred Nobel. He made 355 inventions out of which dynamite was the most famous. Around 8 years before Alfred Nobel died; a French newspaper published his obituary by mistake. It said 'The merchant of death is dead.' This was not how Alfred wanted to be remembered after his death! So he wrote a will. A will is a document that talks about who will get a person's wealth after his death. His will said that his wealth should be given away every year to people who make an important contribution to mankind. That is how the Nobel Prize came into existence after his death in 1896.

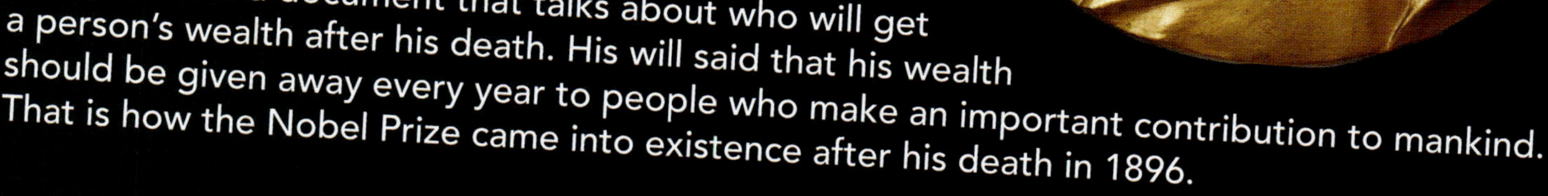

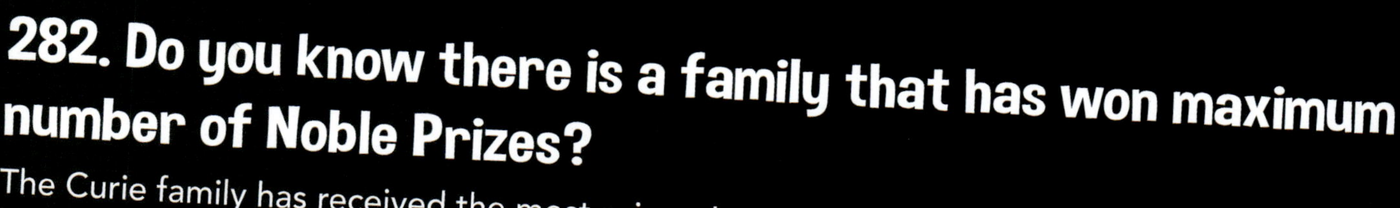

282. Do you know there is a family that has won maximum number of Noble Prizes?

The Curie family has received the most prizes. Let's see the details - Marie Skłodowska-Curie received the prizes in Physics (in 1903) and Chemistry (in 1911).

Her husband, Pierre Curie, shared the 1903 Physics prize with her.

Their daughter, Irène Joliot-Curie, received the Chemistry Prize in 1935 together with her husband Frédéric Joliot-Curie.

283. When was the first e-mail sent?

Ray Tomlinson invented the whole idea of e-mail in 1971. He was working as a computer engineer with a company named Bolt Beranek and Newman (BBN). This was the company hired by the United States Defence Department to build the first Internet in 1968. No one asked Ray to invent such a thing. He was working on a different program that took care of 'local' messaging when this idea clicked him. The first email he sent was from one computer to another, which was lying next to each other.

284. Who invented the internet?

Unlike other inventions, there is no single inventor of the internet. Many scientists and engineers worked together to build what we today know as the internet.

Unlike email, the idea of the internet developed because of a need. In 1957, the Soviet Union (now Russia) launched its space shuttle, Sputnik. The Americans felt that they should not lag behind in science and technology. Lots of money was invested to launch programs that involved research and technological development. The Americans were also scared that the Soviet Union may attack them or disrupt their telephone lines. That is how the idea of having a system to communicate by sitting far away was needed. The system of ARPANET was first created that eventually developed into what we know as the internet.

Today, we can send mails, share pictures, exchange videos with so many people in any corner of the world because of the internet. You can find any information on the internet.

285. If we have to find any information on internet, it pops up in a minute? How is that possible?

When we have to find any information on the internet, we take the help of search engines. The search engines find out information on the world wide web (www). Now search engines have an army of many 'spiders'. The moment you type a question, the spiders run very fast towards pages, known as web pages, which have that question or words similar to it. Searching by the spiders is called 'crawling'. How fast the spiders can 'crawl' on the page decides how good or fast that search engine is.

286. Who invented the first search engine?

Before search engines such as google, bing, yahoo, etc. came, a tool was created by a student named Alan Emtage. He was a computer science student at McGill University in Montreal. He called her search engine 'Archie'. It actually meant archive but the 'v' was missing. Archive means a place or a store with documents that explain about a group of people, place or a building. But Archie could only search files among limited data. It needed improvement. Then came search engines 'Veronica' and 'Jughead'.

It was in 1993 that Matthew Gray invented the first search engine that could search the web pages. It was called the world wide web wanderer!

287. What is www?

WWW stands for the world wide web. Imagine the web of a spider. Do you see thin threads that are interlinked to each other and form a web? Just like a web, various documents or files known as web pages are linked to each other. These pages can be seen or accessed through the internet. Various web sites are linked on www. With the help of a web browser or a search engine we can see various pictures, images, information, videos of various websites.

288. Was all this possible without the invention of computer? So when was the first computer invented?

In 1882, Charles Babbage wondered why is it so complicated to calculate and solve math problems. So he decided to build a machine that could do calculations and solve math problems automatically. He called it the Babbage Machine. This machine became the basis of what we today know as a computer. So, even if he did not set out to create a computer, he invented a machine that worked like a computer. From then on, many people improved on the invention and today we have sleek, fast, digital computers!

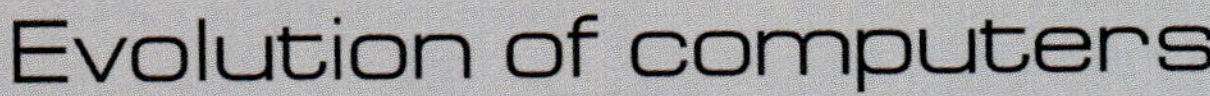
Evolution of computers

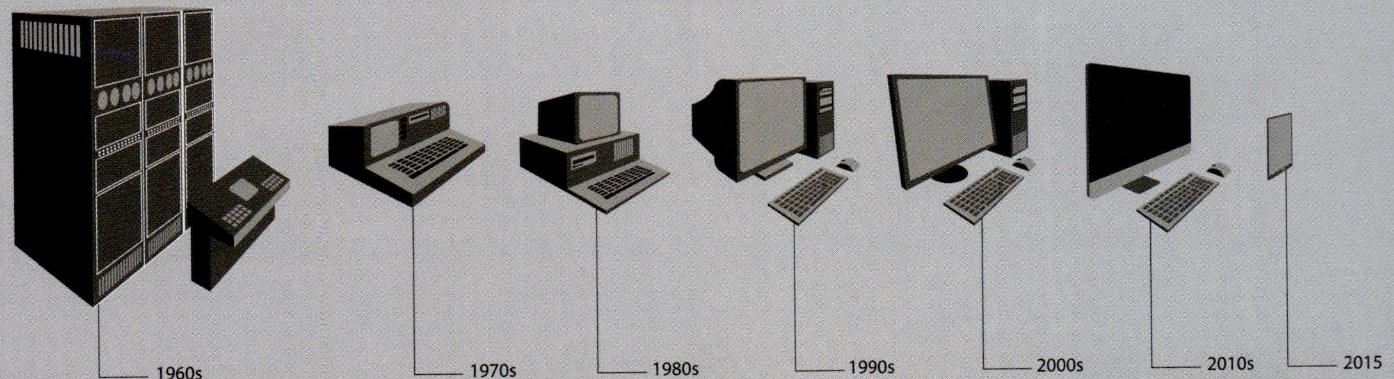

289. Bill Gates didn't invent the computer or the email or www. So what is his contribution to computer?

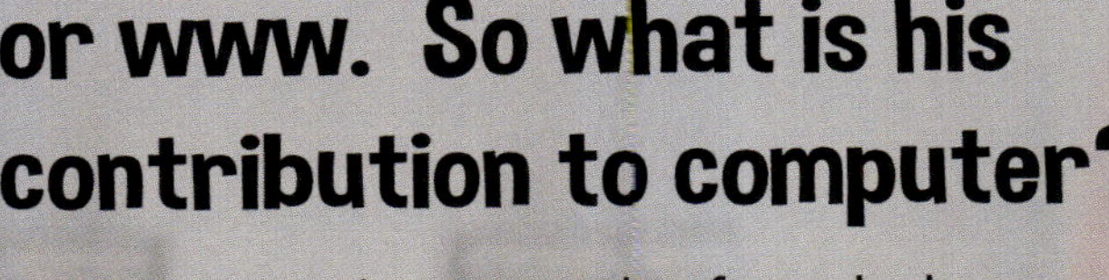

Bill Gates is the man who founded Microsoft, a software company with Paul Allen in 1976. This company became the largest manufacturers of personal computers. Like Henry Ford revolutionised the car industry, Bill Gates made the personal computer reach every home.

Bill Gates wrote the first software program at the age of 13. With the help of a group of friends he created a software for school's payroll system. He then dropped out of Harvard with his friend Paul Allen to form Microsoft.

290. What is Steve Jobs famous for?

Steve Jobs started a revolution in computers. On April Fool's Day, in 1976 he formed a software company called Apple along with Steve Wozniak and Ronald Wayne. He was an inventor and an entrepreneur with a great vision. He was the one who brought out the range of i-pod, i-pad, i-phone. The products of Apple have such finish and quality that the people love all its products. Fortune, a business magazine, named Apple as the most admired company in 2008 and the most loved in the world from 2008-2012.

Steve Jobs was someone who never settled for anything mediocre. Whatever he wanted to do, he wanted to do it perfectly. That is why Apple products are of such high quality and it is considered the best brand in computers.

291. Who created facebook?

Facebook is a place on the net where people get to chat, comment, post photographs and make new friends from all over the world.

This is called a social networking website. Facebook has over one billion active users from all over the world. It was founded by Mark Zuckerberg along with his classmates at Harvard University in 2004. It was first open to the students of Harvard but soon it was expanded to other universities and colleges. Today, anybody above 13 years can use facebook.

292. What is Wikipedia?

Wikipedia is like an online encyclopedia available for free! It is one of the world's largest encyclopedias which has information about every topic. If you have to search for any topic related to plant, animal, universe, vehicle, books, movies or anything, you will find information on Wikipedia. It was created in 2001 by Jimmy Wales. It is considered to be a very reliable source of information.

293. What is YouTube?

YouTube is a place on the web where you can watch videos and also upload (post) your own videos. Since the videos are on the web, people all over the world can watch them. People can also share their comments on whether they liked or didn't like a video. YouTube was invented by Steve Chen, Chad Hurley and Jawed Karim. They sold their invention to Google and became millionaires.

You can find videos on every topic you can think of, for example, music, cartoons, movies, history, news, events, T.V. shows and much more. If you want to learn anything, there is a video for that too! Have you ever seen your mom watching how to make a new dish on YouTube? Why don't you ask your mom to show you a video on how to make great sketches?

294. What made Nelson Mandela one of the greatest leaders?

Nelson Mandela was born in South Africa at a time when the white Africans ruled the country. Non-white people were not allowed to use libraries, toilets, beaches and parks. Black people could not go with white people to school or play sports with them. This practice of segregation (separation) was called apartheid.

Nelson Mandela opposed apartheid. He spent 27 years in the prison fighting for racial equality (equality for people of all colours of skin). He was released from prison in 1990 due to pressure from prominent international leaders. He became the president of South Africa in 1994 and served till 1999. Thanks to him, today apartheid is no longer practiced in South Africa. Everyone in South Africa has an equal opportunity at work and at home to live the life they want to live.

Who is another freedom fighter who also has a connection with South Africa?

295. People with vision can read by seeing. But what about the blind who cannot see?

They read and write by touch. Braille is a system of reading and writing for those who can't see. The alphabet, numbers and punctuation marks are written in the form of a symbol. The symbol is made out of dots that are raised or embossed. The person can touch and run his/her finger on the letters to read what is written.

Abbreviations have been made to make reading easier. Blind people have to learn these abbreviations which are not a problem for them at all. Braille is written on heavy paper so that the dots can be embossed comfortably. That is why books are bulky.

Braille was first developed in the late 1820s by a young Frenchman named Louis Braille. He was just about eighteen years old when he developed Braille. Because of his creation, the blind all over the world can today get a proper education. Hats off to Louis Braille!

296. Who was Helen Keller?

Helen Keller was a woman of great courage and determination. She was born like a normal baby. But at the age of around one and a half, she lost her eyesight and hearing power in a high fever. But she didn't let her disabilities come in her way. She became an author and inspired other people with disabilities.

Later, Helen wrote many books, raised money to help people with disabilities and travelled widely. And you know what, she loved dogs!

297. Can you believe that Hitler who caused so much of destruction was a very creative man?

Hitler was a man with a short height and a short moustache but he caused a big war-World War II. He was the one who first used the atom bomb on people and cities of Hiroshima and Nagasaki in Japan which were completely destroyed. It is hard to believe that Hitler always wanted to be an artist. He was fond of painting, drawing and arts. He moved to Vienna and did watercolour painting. He sold postcards to earn some money. He applied in the Academy of Fine Arts twice but was rejected. His father did not support him in his career as an artist.

It was in one of the political meetings that Hitler gave a speech. His powerful voice attracted attention from everyone. From then, there was no looking back. He joined the Nazi party and soon became its leader. Through his speeches, he convinced the people that he would make Germany rise in the whole of Europe. He was elected the Chancellor of Germany in 1933. Later he turned into a dictator who ruled Germany with a firm hand.

298. Who created the cartoon 'Mickey Mouse'?

Walt Disney was the man who created Mickey Mouse that is so popular among children. It was the first cartoon character created and loved by all. Walt Disney grew up in a farm and lived with animals. He spent a lot of time observing and making sketches of the animals.

When he grew up, he started working with an advertising agency. One day lots of mice came into his office. He trapped 10 mice and kept them in a cage. Walt Disney was very unhappy with his work and wanted to be successful. He decided to quit and go to Hollywood. The night before he was to leave, he decided to set all the mice free. 9 mice ran away but one mouse stood there staring at him. That night was the birth of Mickey Mouse!

Why don't you draw a cartoon character out of your imagination and give him a name of your choice?

299. Who created the character of Harry Potter?

J.K Rowling is a British author who created and imagined the character of Harry Potter. Rowling was travelling from Manchester to London in 1990. The train was delayed by 4 hours. In a sudden rush, the idea of a bespectacled boy who attends a wizardly school came to her. She looked for a pen but couldn't find one. In a way it was good. She kept thinking about the characters and did not write at all. The more she thought about it, the clearer all the characters and situations formed in her mind. She began writing her first Harry Potter book 'Philosopher's Stone' later that very day. But it took her many years to complete it as she lost her mother and divorced her husband during that period. Rowling was jobless and had a baby to take care of. In 1995, she finally completed her book. 12 publishers rejected it till one agreed to publish Harry Potter. Today, Harry potter is a rage and J.K.Rowling is a millionaire all because of her determination!

300. Who is the first African American President of America?

Barack Obama is the first African American to become the President of United States of America. He was born in Hawaii. His mother was from Kansas while his father was born in Kenya, Africa. After his parents were divorced, his mother married a man from Indonesia and the family moved to Indonesia. Later, Barack returned to Hawaii and was raised by his grandparents. He was raised on scholarships and loans. He went to Harvard Law School to study law.

Later he decided to join politics. He was an excellent speaker and was popular. In 2008, he defeated Hillary Clinton to become the Democratic candidate for president. He moved on to defeat the Republican candidate, John McCain to become the 44th President of the United States in 2009. Did you know he loves to play basketball? In fact, he was a very good basket - ball player and was nicknamed "Barry O' Bomber" at high school.

301. Do you know that Leonardo Da Vinci was a painter, a scientist, a philosopher and an inventor?

Leonardo Da Vinci is called a universal genius. Let's find out why!

He painted some masterpieces like Mona Lisa and The Last supper.

He made sketches and researched on various machines like submarine, tank, calculator, glider and many more.

He was also a scientist who studied anatomy (study of body) and various principles of mathematics.

He was a philosopher who expressed his ideas and thoughts about life through his paintings.

302. Butterflies and moths look very similar. In fact they do have some similarities.

They both are insects and have wings.

Their wings are covered with tiny scales. If you touch a butterfly or moth, you will feel some dust on your hand. The dust is actually their tiny scales.

They have a long tongue which is curled inside the mouth. It is uncurled and is used as a drinking straw to suck nectar from the flowers.

They have antennae attached to their heads. They are thin wire-like organs that help these insects to smell and control their flying.

303. So, how can we tell moths and butterflies apart? Do we simply have to look really carefully to spot the difference?

Butterflies have long, smooth antennae while the moths have hairy ones. Butterflies have round bulb at the end of their antennae while moths don't have it.

Butterflies fly in the daytime and while resting they keep their wings folded up over their bodies. Moths fly at night and when they rest their wings lie flat on either side.

Butterflies are larger and have bright-coloured patterns on their wings while moths are smaller with dull-coloured wings.

304. Do you know moths and butterflies have similar lifecycle too with only one small difference?

Like many insects, moths and butterflies go through four stages in their life:

Egg: Adult moths and butterflies lay eggs on leaves. Eggs hatch into caterpillars, also known as larva.

Larva (more than one is larvae): Larvae grow rapidly, so they need to eat a lot too. They are always hungry and feed on leaves around them. They shed their skins many times.

Pupa (more than one is pupae): The larvae grip onto a leaf or bark and make a cocoon around them and hide inside. Inside the cocoon, the larvae are changing. They are now pupae. Butterflies make chrysalis while moths make cocoons.

Adult: Pupae emerge out of their cocoons or chrysalis as adults. The adult butterfly or moth then finds a mate so they can lay more eggs. The whole cycle starts all over again!

305. Why do moths need to make cocoons?

As you have seen, these insects go through many big changes while growing into adults. Their bodies take on new shapes at each stage! Their legs are changing and they often lose the ability to move around for a brief time. Also, they need all their energy to help them grow and change. What do you think would happen if they are just sitting on a leaf or on a branch? Birds and other insects may come along and attack them. So, they make a cocoon around their bodies to remain safe. It is the same reason why butterflies make chrysalis. Did you know that silk is made from these cocoons?

306. Why do moths make hole in our clothes?

We have heard that moths eat our clothes and make holes in them. But wait! Actually it's not moths but their tiny larvae that eat your clothes. The larvae need to eat a lot to grow rapidly and become a mature adult. They need protein that is present in the fibres of the natural fabric. These fabrics are made from animal fibres and contain a protein called keratin. So, female moths choose fabrics made from animal fibres to lay their eggs, so that when they hatch, the hungry caterpillars can feed on the protein.

307. Have you ever seen grown-ups keeping moth balls with your clothes? Why do you think they do this?

Mothballs are small balls made up of some very harsh chemicals. When exposed to air, these chemicals are released as fumes or gas. This sharp smelling gas is toxic and kills the larvae. This smell is bad for us too as it can cause allergies. They should be kept away from the reach of children as they are poisonous. The good news is that special herb sachets are now available that can work as effectively to keep moths away from your woollens. They are not poisonous and smell lovely too.

308. How is fabric made?

Fabric is made of fibres. These fibres are first spun together to make yarns which in turn are made into different types of fabrics by weaving, knitting, felting or crocheting. So, where does this fibre come from? It comes from plants (cotton, linen), animals (leather, wool, silk) and are even made by man (rayon, polyester, nylon). When it comes from plants and animals it is called natural fabric and when it is man-made, we call it synthetic fabric.

309. Where does cotton come from? How is it made into fabric?

Cotton is a hair-like fibre that grows on shrubby plants. These plants first grow white flowers that fall off and are replaced by small green pods called bolls. Inside the pods or bolls, cotton fibres grow. These pods burst in two-three months, revealing white puffballs of cotton! The cotton can now be picked either using machines or by hand. It is now ready to be processed in industrial looms where the puffs are spun into yarn and then woven into fabrics to make your favourite clothing. Australia and Egypt produce the highest quality cottons in the world.

310. Are cotton puffs inside the pods always white?

No, cotton also comes in other natural colours such as green, brown, red and tan. But this naturally coloured cotton has smaller fibres than the white cotton. The small-fibred cotton is difficult to process in the looms; therefore it was not used often earlier. The natural-coloured varieties grew almost extinct until some brown cotton seeds were discovered by a scientist Sally Fox. She did some experiments and used technology to grow long-fibred coloured cotton which is known as FoxFibre.

311. How is linen made?

Linen is one of the oldest and most expensive textiles in the world. It is made from the fibres of flax plants. Flax plants produce beautiful purple flowers with fibrous stems. These stems are made into tough, durable threads. Linen is the strongest of the vegetable fibres and is two to three times stronger than cotton. It is known for its lightweight, cool feel even in extremely hot weather. It doesn't cause any skin-allergies, repels insects and protects from harmful UV rays.

312. How is silk made?

Silk is the most beautiful of all the natural fibres. It is made by silkworms. In fact, silkworms are not worms at all; they are actually caterpillars or larvae of a moth. There is a special moth called 'Bombyx Mori'. It goes through an amazing lifecycle that has four stages starting from an egg. It then becomes a larva or caterpillar and then turns into a pupa before becoming finally a moth. It's the larva (called a silkworm) that makes a cocoon. It feeds on mulberry leaves and secretes a sticky protein from its body to make this cocoon. This cocoon is then collected and is processed with lots of hard work and care to make yarns of silk.

313. Do you know that making silk actually harms the silkworms?

We know that cocoons are collected and processed to make silks. But what would happen if we leave the cocoons just like that? The silkworm inside becomes a pupa and will come out of the cocoon by chewing the cocoon strands. This process damages the cocoon as the silk strands would be shorter and less silk will be made out of it. So, in the silk industry, cocoons are dropped in boiling water before the moth can actually come out on its own. Did you know that 15 silkworms are killed to get 1 gram of silk and 1500 silkworms are killed to get one metre of woven silk cloth!

314. We all find pearls beautiful. Have you ever wondered how they are made?

Pearls are the only gemstone made by living animals. They are made by a group of water animals called mollusks. Yeah, it's a strange-sounding name but ever heard of oysters, clams or mussels? They all are mollusks.

All mollusks with the shell can make pearls. When a foreign object like a grain of sand or stone gets inside the shell by chance, the mollusk covers it with a mineral to protect itself. This mineral comes from the inner lining of the shell. The mollusk continues to cover the object with many layers of this mineral, finally forming a pearl! These are called natural pearls and are very rarely found in nature. Hence, many mollusks need to be gathered, opened and therefore, killed to find a natural pearl. There are cultured pearls too.

315. How are cultured pearls made?

Cultured pearls are made or harvested in pearl farms. To make cultured pearls, an oyster is gently opened and some grain of dust is placed inside its shell so that it can start making the pearl. Did you just see how this is similar to making a natural pearl? Only here, a foreign object is placed inside the shell on purpose. A natural pearl is made when it happens by chance. This way, people can make as many pearls as they want to and it does not kill the mollusk.

Japan and China are known for making cultured pearls. Pearls coming from these countries are called Akoya Pearls. These pearls are made by saltwater oysters. They are famous for their shine and beauty and are usually white or cream in colour. They sometimes have light shades of pink or silver too.

316. Do you know not all pearls are considered gemstones?

Yes, not all pearls are gemstones. Pearls made of freshwater mussels and saltwater oysters are regarded as gemstones. Have you noticed the special shine on a pearl? The shiny outer layer of the pearl comes from the mineral that is present inside the inner lining of the shell of the mollusks. This mineral covers the grain of sand so that it can't irritate the mollusk. This mineral is called nacre or mother of pearl. It is produced only by oysters and mussels. The pearls made by clams and other mollusks are not shiny as they don't produce a nacre in their shell. These pearls are, therefore, not considered as gemstones.

Do you know how big the largest pearl in the world is? It is 24 cm in diameter and weighs around 14 pounds. It is called Pearl of Lao Tzu or the Pearl of Allah and was found in Philippines. It was made inside a clam. So, it is not considered as a gemstone but it is a pearl nevertheless.

317. Are all pearls white and round?

All pearls are unique. Not all pearls are white or even round for that matter. They come in many shapes like oval and irregular, and in many colours too such as gold, purple, pink, grey, yellow and even black! They take their colour from the mineral found in the inside of the shell.

318. What gemstone is called a girl's best friend? It is diamond.

Diamonds are minerals made up of carbon. They are formed very deep under the Earth (around 150-200 kilometres down) where the heat and pressure turn the carbon into diamonds. In fact, it takes billions of years for the carbon to become diamonds. Most diamonds found in nature are between one to three billion years old. That is why they are so expensive.

319. So, how are these diamonds extracted from deep down the Earth?

Diamonds are found in different places around the world. They are found even under the floor of oceans. Diamonds are brought to the surface through mining. Volcanic eruptions create long pipes within the earth. People dig tunnels in these pipes to bring rocks to the surface. These rocks contain diamonds. Another way is to mine diamonds from sand beaches or from the river beds. Most of the Earth's natural diamond deposits are found in Africa. Some of the other largest diamond-producing countries include Australia, Congo and Russia.

320. Can anyone go in these mines? Are they open to public?

The Crater of Diamonds State Park in Arkansas (The United States of America) is the only diamond mine in the world that is open to the public. You can dig for free and what's more, you can keep any diamond you find, big or small. Now that sounds awesome!! Did you know that America is the largest buyer of diamonds in the world?

321. Do you know only 20% of mined diamonds are used for jewellery?

It is because not all the diamonds that are found are of very good quality or gem quality. Only high-quality diamonds have good shine. These are the ones that are fit for making jewellery pieces. 80% of the diamonds are used for industrial purposes. They are the hardest known natural substance. So, they are used to make equipment or to cut other hard materials or to drill into solid surfaces in industries and in laboratories.

322. Are all diamonds colourless?

A diamond is usually pale yellow to colourless but it can also be coloured. Yellow and brown are the most common coloured diamonds while blue and red diamonds are found very rarely. There are green, orange, red and even black-coloured diamonds. A diamond gets its colour due to the impurities present in it. A colourless diamond will have more value as it has no impurities.

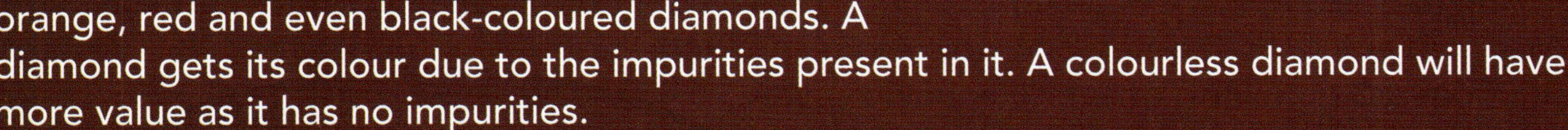

323. Gold is very commonly used in jewellery too but is it really common?

Gold is a rare and precious element that is found deep within the Earth's surface. Its bright, yellow colour and shine give it a beautiful appearance. While most metals are white or gray in colour, gold is one of the only two metals that are not white. The other one is copper. Scientists tell us that so far we have only taken out 20% of the total gold from the Earth. Most gold has been found in the U.S., Canada, South Africa, China, Russia, and Chile.

324. Where does gold come from?

Yes, we know it is found deep down the Earth's surface but there are many amazing theories about how gold came to Earth. Some scientists believe that gold came from outer space. It sounds like science fiction but scientists who study earth science have proved that billions of years ago, there was a meteoric shower on Earth and these meteorites contained gold.

Another theory says that gold actually came from a collision. It happened when dead neutron stars bumped into each other with extraordinary great force. It led to the explosion of gold dust on Earth. Take your pick what you want to believe.

And don't get surprised if the theories keep changing. Our scientists are a curious lot. With new technologies and tools, they are ready to explore new ideas and come up with new, amazing discoveries every once in a while.

325. How is gold found in nature? Is it lying around in solid clumps or flakes?

Gold is mostly found as grains or crystals and sometimes as gold nuggets too. The largest gold nugget ever found is named the "Welcome Stranger". It was 10 by 25 inches and produced 2,248 ounces of gold. It was discovered in Australia and was found just two inches below the ground surface. There are other famous gold nuggets too, such as Hand of Faith.

Would you like to have gold nuggets in breakfast? Well, that's silly! Who eats gold?

It might sound strange but it is edible. It is not toxic. In some countries, gold flakes are used to decorate sweets and other food items. In old times, centuries ago, the dust of pure gold was actually used in medicines. Even today, it is used in treating many diseases.

326. Let's discover some golden facts about gold that makes it a truly special metal.

Unlike other metals, gold is not affected by air, water and chemicals. Hence, it keeps its shine even after thousands of years.

It is the most ductile metal on Earth. This means it is very easily made into thin wires. 1 ounce (28 grams) of gold can be made to stretch over 50 miles.

It is also malleable. This means it can be very easily hammered into thin sheets. A thin sheet of gold can be almost transparent.

Gold is an excellent reflector of heat. This is why it is used in spacecraft to reflect harmful solar radiations.

Did you know The Royal Bank Plaza building in Toronto, Canada has special 14,000 windows coated with a thin layer of gold! This coating keeps the building warm in winters and cool in summers by reflecting heat radiations.

327. Do you know that 100% pure gold is so soft that it can be moulded with hands? In fact, it can be made as thin as a sewing thread. But if pure gold is so soft, how is jewellery made out of it?

More than half of the gold that has been taken out of the Earth is used for making jewellery. But absolutely pure gold cannot be used to make jewellery or gold coins. It has to be mixed with other metals like silver and copper to make it hard.

328. Where does silver come from?

Silver is a beautiful metal with a brilliant white shine. It is found naturally with gold. It is also found in rocks in combination with other metals such as copper and lead. These rocks are called ores. (For example, you can say silver is often found in copper and lead ores). It is a soft metal but harder than gold. Most of the silver in the world comes from United States, Mexico, Canada, Peru, Russia and Australia. More than 95% of silver is used for industrial and decorative uses, for example, photography and jewellery and silverware.

329. Do you know that the country Argentina is named after a chemical element? Any guesses what is the name of this element?

In Latin language, Silver is called Argentum. Its chemical symbol, Ag, is derived from this name itself. Argentina is the only country that is named after a chemical element. It is because silver is found here in abundance. Argentina adopted the name after it got its independence from Spain in 1815. Before this, it was called the Viceroyalty of Rio de la Plata (river of silver). That is a complicated but a fun name. The word Argentum also has its roots with the Sanskrit word Arjuna which means white.

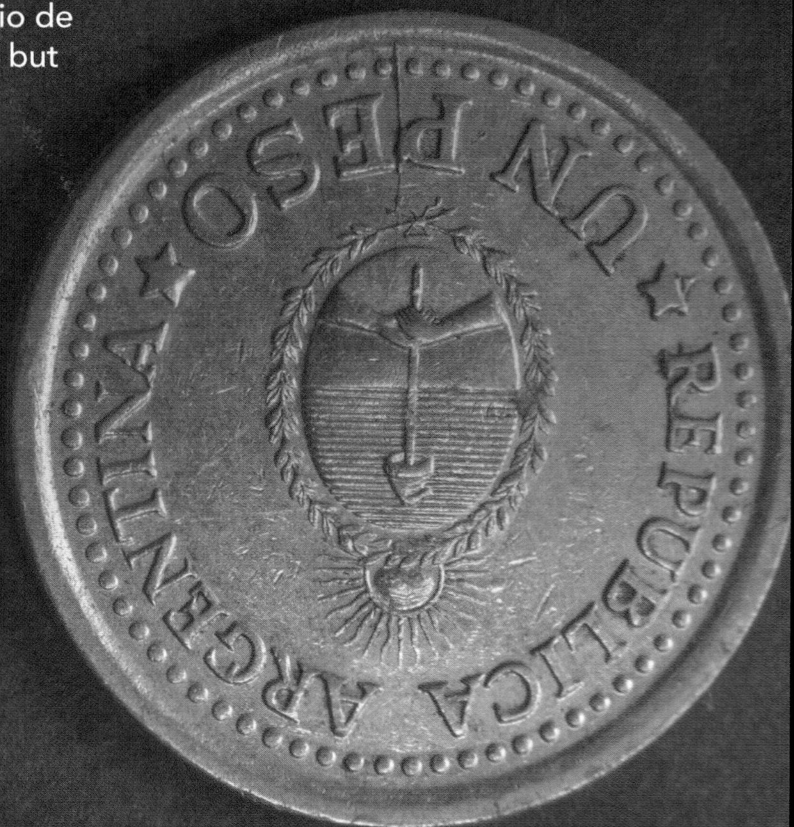

330. What makes silver so special?

Next to gold, it is the second most malleable and ductile metal on Earth.

Silver's whiteness makes it the most reflective of all the elements. When it is polished, it can reflect almost 100 percent of the light. This makes it the best element for making mirrors used in telescopes.

It has amazing medicinal properties. It's a natural antibiotic and kills bacteria. Because of silver's germ-killing properties, it was considered that children who were fed with silver spoons were typically healthier babies.

Silver is also utilised in batteries for portable surgical tools, hearing aids and space travel.

A chemical made from silver (silver iodide) is often used in making artificial clouds to produce rain. This process is called cloud seeding.

Oh, wait! There is another thing that makes silver very special. The word silver is one of the few words in the English language that is nearly impossible to rhyme.

331. What is sterling silver?

It is the name given to a special silver that is not 100 % silver. Sterling silver is only 92.5% silver. It is added with other metals, usually copper to give it more strength. It is often used for jewellery, silverware and decorations.

332. How are crayons made?

Crayons are made of paraffin wax and colour. The wax is heated and the pigment which gives colour to it is added. Then, the liquid is put into moulds that give shape to the crayon. Once it cools down, the crayon is ready. Nowadays, since children put crayons in mouth, more and more natural colours are being used.

The first set of crayons was made in 1903 in basic colours red, blue, green, etc. It was made of charcoal and colour. Paraffin wax was discovered later. Today, crayons are available in various colours, glitter and fragrances.

333. How are perfumes made?

Perfumes are used to make clothes, bodies, rooms and cosmetics smell better. Perfumes are made from natural oils that can be extracted from plants and animals. Fragrances like sandalwood, lavender, lemon, jasmine, all are made out of natural oils extracted out of plants. Fragrances like musk are obtained from musk deer. Besides natural oils, perfumes are also made by using synthetic oils extracted from petroleum and natural gas known as petrochemicals.

There are various categories of perfumes. Some last longer while some don't. Actually, the oil extract is mixed with alcohol to make a perfume. Alcohol evaporates very quickly and helps to spread the fragrance of the oil in the air too. If more alcohol is used to dilute the perfume, it is called toilet water or cologne. It is less lasting than perfume. Interestingly, the same perfume smells differently on different bodies.

334. Why does the same perfume smells different on different bodies?

Our skin is made of various chemicals, for example oil and hormones. Every person's body has these chemicals in different quantities. When we sweat, these chemicals are released in the air and this gives our sweat some kind of smell. We call this body odour. Everyone has their unique body odour. Now, when we apply perfume to our skin, the oils in the perfume combines with the chemicals in the skin and releases a unique fragrance.

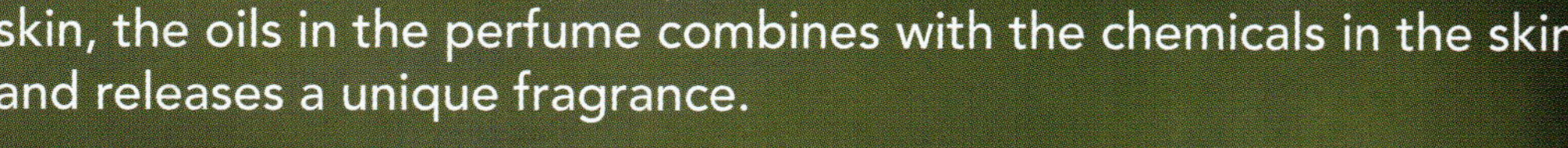

335. Why are plants green?

The leaves have a green pigment called chlorophyll. This makes the plants green. But what does chlorophyll do? Chlorophyll, along with sun and water, makes the food for the plant. Take a leaf and observe it closely. You will see thin thread-like structures in the leaf. These are like thin pipes that carry water and food to the entire leaf. Plants that don't have leaves cannot make food of their own.

336. Is mushroom a plant?

There are many types of fungi. Some fungi make you sick by giving you infections while some are healthy, for example:

Mushrooms: They are edible fungi. But we only eat a few types of mushrooms as not all mushrooms are edible.

Toadstools: These are brightly-coloured mushrooms and poisonous to eat.

Yeast: It is used to make bread.

Mold: It is the fuzzy green growth that we see on old bread or old food. It is poisonous and can make us very sick.

337. If fungi can't make their own food, how do they get their food?

Fungi can feed on anything living or dead. It can grow in soil, on plants or on old food. It feeds on living or dead organisms by decomposing them into smaller units. They produce long, thin threads which are called hyphae. Hyphae spread through the food and release enzymes to break down the food into substances that the fungi can easily absorb. This is how fungi get their nutrition, that is, by rotting the materials around them.

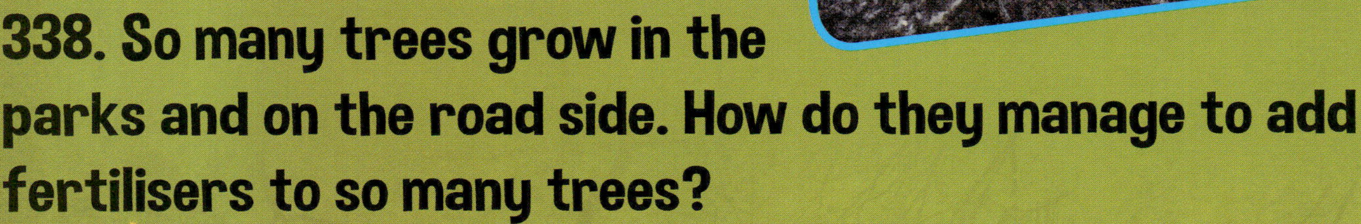

338. So many trees grow in the parks and on the road side. How do they manage to add fertilisers to so many trees?

Leaves that fall from the trees act like natural fertiliser. They gradually get absorbed into the soil by the water, get decomposed and become a fertiliser. This way there is no need to add fertilisers regularly. They can be added from time-to-time. Hence, the leaves that fall near the trees and in the garden should not be removed. Nature should be allowed to follow its own path!

339. Why do gardeners plough the garden?

With the help of a spade, the gardener turns the soil so that it can 'breathe'. It is believed that ploughing helps the plants to grow as more carbon dioxide is available from the soil. But there is a problem with this method. When the soil is turned, the weeds, sleeping quietly below the surface of the soil, wake up. After ploughing they begin to grow as well and then we begin with the process of weeding!

In real terms, ploughing may not be required at all. The earthworms and other insects in the soil are natural gardeners which keep turning the soil.

When large fields or farms are ploughed, the natural microbes like fungi, bacteria present in the soil also tend to get killed. It is these microbes who make the soil healthy for growth by adding nutrients to it.

340. Why do plants need water? How do we know how much water they need?

Plants make their own food using nutrients from the soil and carbon dioxide from the air. Water helps the plants to absorb nutrients from the soil and transport it to all parts of the plant. How much water a plant need varies from plant to plant. Some plants with fleshy leaves like aloe vera, cactus, ponytail palm, etc. need less water.

The best way to judge if you need to water your plants is by pressing 3 inches deep in the soil (which may be as long as your forefinger!). If the soil is wet and soft, you need not add water. But if it appears dry, lift your watering can and pour some water. Ouch! Remember to pour water on the soil and not on the plant.

341. Why do we need a watering can and not give water with a pipe?

Think. Do you take a bath with a shower or your mom opens a pipe and aims it at you? Sounds funny, right? But try it once. You will find that the pressure of water from the pipe is a little hurting. Similarly for plants growing in the garden soil or in a pot should not be watered with a pipe. A sprinkler placed in the garden or a watering can showers water gently on all the plants. Also if you pour water from a pipe, the sudden rush of water can remove the soil around the roots of the plant. Exposing the roots can damage and kill the plant. You need to be sensitive and gentle with plants; they are living things like us!

342. What will happen if we give too much water to the plants?

There are different kinds of soil found in different places. All types of soil have pores. These pores contain oxygen. When there is excess water, the pores get clogged. No oxygen is available to the plant. It is like not being able to breathe when you are drowning in water. Similarly, the plant is unable to breathe and can die. The roots can rot and the plant can wither away.

If you lift one of the pots in your garden or balcony, you will find a tiny hole on the bottom of the pot. This hole is made so that the excess water is drained. Similarly, the drainage system is built-in gardens so that water doesn't remain stagnant. There are places where plants are planted on a raised ground so that water doesn't accumulate around the plant.

343. What happens to the water that doesn't get absorbed by the plant?

Let's find that out with the help of an experiment.

Step 1: Water the plant well using a watering can. Remember, you need to water the plant at the base and not the stems.

Step 2: Place a large, transparent plastic bag over the plant. Take care that you do not damage the leaves. Tape the bag tightly around the pot. Leave the plant overnight.

Step 3: Look at the plant the next day. Inside the bag, water vapour released by the plant turns back into the water. The air inside is warm and moist, like the air in a rainforest.

Excess water not needed by the plant evaporates back into the air in the form of water vapour. This process is called transpiration.

344. We have seen gardeners sow seeds of special flowers and plants. But who plants so many trees in the forest?

Forests grow on their own. Yes! Each tree has a fruit or a flower that has seeds. These seeds fall on the ground and in that place grows a new tree! That is how trees after trees grow. Birds also carry the seeds far. That's why it is amazing to see an unusual tree at a place because some bird carried its seeds in its beak and dropped it there. Animals also break the fruits and in the process seeds drop on the ground. Leaves that fall on the ground act as natural fertilisers and so does the waste excreted by animals! These help the tree to get nutrition and grow.

345. How can we know how old is a tree?

Now, this is simple. It will be best understood if you first go and observe a fallen or a cut tree. You will notice rings on the cut tree trunk. These are called annual rings. If there are 25 rings, the age of the tree is 25. In each growth season, the tree adds wood on its trunk. If you observe more closely, the rings and the pattern also indicate the changes in growth and area during the life span of a tree.

346. Why do some flowers smell good?

The sweet fragrance of the flower is to attract the bees, butterflies and other insects. These insects carry the pollen of one flower to other flowers. Pollen is the powdery substance found in all flowers of the plant. It is produced naturally by the flower. It is the pollen from which the plants reproduce. So, the plant has to attract these agents to carry their pollen. Some pollen is also carried by wind but flowers also need bees and butterflies to spread their glory far and wide!

The colourful petals of the flower don't have any function. They are there to attract the bees and the butterflies!

347. Do you know there are plants that are carnivorous?

Imagine an insect crawling up the leaf of a plant. In a second, the leaf shuts and traps the insects. When it opens, there is no insect! The plant has swallowed it up. Yes, this is true. There is such a plant called Venus Fly Trap. Like animals, there are plants that are carnivorous.

There are other plants like a pitcher plant. It is called pitcher because it looks like a pitcher full of nectar. Insects get attracted to take a sip from the pitcher and fall into a trap. There are many other carnivorous plants that use different techniques to trap their victims.

Carnivorous plants grow in soil that doesn't provide enough nutrition. They have to depend on insects, flies, rodents for their food.

348. Do you know that there are plants that are parasites?

Firstly, do you know what a parasite is? A parasite is an organism that lives inside another organism called the host. A parasite eats from the host and gradually, makes the host weak. Not a good thing to do, right?

There are plants that are parasites. These are of two types:

Partial parasites - These plants take partially from the host. They take water from the host but make their own food. Like mistletoe plant. It digs its roots into the host plant to take out water to complete the process of photosynthesis.

Total parasites - These wrap themselves around the host plant and grow very fast. Gradually, the host plant dies and the parasite plant moves on to another host. These plants generally don't have roots or stems and grow on the host plant. Rafflesia Cantleyi is one such example. It is a bad-smelling plant. It smells like rotten flesh and is also known as a corpse flower. This smell attracts the flies which pollinates the plant. This huge rubbery flower can be bigger than 3 ft and of course steals everything from the host.

349. Can a tree grow in a pot?

Bonsai in Japanese means tree in a pot. It is a Japanese art of growing a miniature tree in a tray or a shallow container. To make a bonsai, you need to invest time and know the art of pruning (cutting). Many techniques are used to grow a tree into a bonsai. The tree is pruned and its branches cut in such a way that it grows normally, looking beautiful like a natural tree. A good bonsai should look like you have picked a tree from a forest and shrunk it very small. All kinds of trees-flowering, non-flowering, fruit-bearing trees are used to make bonsai. Some of the trees are like pine, plum, cherry, etc.

350. There are mounds of soil and mud in the garden. Are they made by termites?

Mounds in the soil are made by many insects and ants, one of them is termites. Termites are also known as white ants. They build their homes in the mud. They dig the ground open and live in the mounds called anthill. They are capable of building large mounds, beginning with tiny hills.

When they make their passage in the ground, it helps to turn the soil and let the air pass. That way they are helpful but when they turn their attention to buildings, they are not so helpful. The termites can also bite through wood and make their homes inside. Their bodies can digest the starch in the wood and this is actually their real diet. So, they can destroy the wood used anywhere in the building and really harm it. Though they are related to cockroaches, they live in large numbers in the form of a colony just like bees and ants.

351. What are those spots on yummy, red, nice-looking strawberries?

Strawberry must be one of your favourite fruit in your drawings, in your smoothies, jam, ice cream and yogurt. Is that right? This yummy tasting and equally yummy looking fruit has some harsh spots on the outside. They are actually the seeds of the strawberry! In fact, strawberry is the fleshy stem of the plant and not really a fruit. The real fruits are actually these tiny yellow seeds on the outside. These seeds are called achene. It sounds similar to the word acne which means pimples on the face! It is full of vitamin C.

Pineapple and cashew fruits also bear seeds on the outside.

352. Is 'Kiwi' a bird or a fruit?

Kiwi is a flightless bird of the size of a chicken. It is the native bird of New Zealand and also the country's national symbol. It is because of this bird that New Zealanders are often referred to as Kiwis.

But kiwi is also the name of a fruit. It is actually a Chinese gooseberry that has its origin in China. Around 1960, New Zealanders began to grow Chinese gooseberries on a large scale. They wanted to name it and market it all around the world. They chose the name kiwi fruit. Interestingly, the fruit resembles the bird which has a round stomach and light brown feathers. From then on, the Chinese gooseberry began to be called Kiwi.

353. We all love chocolates. It is one of the most popular sweets in the world. But where does chocolate come from?

Well, believe it or not, chocolate does grows on trees. Chocolate is made from cocoa beans which grow on cacao trees. Cacao trees grow in Africa, Central and South America and parts of Asia, where the weather is hot. The tree grows pods that contain 30-50 bitter beans or seeds. These seeds wouldn't taste very good if you try to eat them! The seeds are sent to factories where they are heated, dried, cleaned, roasted and crushed. What is left behind is a gooey, dark brown paste known as cocoa liquor. It is mixed with sugar, vanilla, milk and sometimes nuts and fruits are also added. It is poured into moulds of different shapes and sizes and is allowed to cool. Your chocolate is now ready to eat!

The first chocolate bars were made in Switzerland in 1819.

354. Where does vanilla come from? Does it come from trees too?

Yes, it sure does. In fact, vanilla comes from a type of orchid plant. It is known as vanilla orchid. It grows vanilla pods that contain beans. They look kind of like dried-up black-coloured string beans! They go through special drying and processing before we get liquid vanilla extract. It is famous for its delicious smell and subtle taste. Do you want to know how it smells like? People describe its smell as spicy, woody, floral and fruity all at once. It is used to make chocolates and also used as a flavouring agent in cakes, cookies and ice creams.

355. Does coffee come from plants too?

What do most grownups look forward to first thing in the morning? Ask them and most will answer that they crave coffee. It is a strong, aromatic drink made from coffee beans. The coffee plant grows small, white flowers and red berries that contain the coffee beans inside! These berries are called cherries. The cherries are picked, cleaned and roasted. Some of the beans are ground before it is sold as a coffee powder at shops. But some of the beans are sold as such as some people like to grind them fresh just when they want to make a cup of coffee. Most of the world's coffee comes from Latin American countries like Brazil, Mexico and Guatemala.

356. Why coffee can be harmful to kids?

It is because coffee contains a chemical called caffeine. If taken in small doses, caffeine makes us more alert and energetic. That is the reason why grownups prefer to drink it in the morning. But in kids even small quantities, if taken regularly, can make kids hyperactive. It can also make it difficult for you to concentrate and may make you fall asleep.

Did you know cold drinks contain caffeine too? But there are other things also that make cold drinks bad for us. They contain chemicals that damage the enamel of the teeth, causing them to become yellow. Cold drinks make our bones weak too. They contain extra sugar that can cause diabetes and make us obese.

357. Rubber bands, car-tyres, pencil erasers, so many things that we use every day are made from rubber. But where does rubber come from?

There are two kinds of rubber—natural and synthetic rubber. Natural rubber comes from the rubber tree. When a slit is made in this tree, thick white liquid oozes out. It is called sap or latex. It is mixed with other chemicals like water and acid to make it thicker, turning it into a natural rubber. It is then dried and formed into thick and thin sheets. Rubber trees are grown in plantations. Countries like Malaysia, Indonesia, and Thailand produce most of the rubber.

358. Did you know not all rubber we use today is made from latex?

Not all rubber we use today is made from latex. It is also manufactured in the industries by a special chemical process. This rubber is called synthetic rubber. Synthetic rubber is much stronger than the natural rubber. It can also tolerate high temperatures making it fit for making automobile tyres. A man named Charles Goodyear is credited for making synthetic rubber for the first time. He worked hard for many years trying to mix so many things together. Finally, he was successful in making strong and weatherproof rubber.

359. Does the word Goodyear sounds familiar to you?

You must have noticed the name imprinted on the tyres of some cars or perhaps during the F1 car racing season. Goodyear is also the name of a tyre and rubber company. Though the company was not formed by either Charles Goodyear or his children, it was formed 40 years after his death by a man called Frank. He named the company to honour the efforts of Goodyear.

360. What is F1?

F1 is the short form for Formula One. It is also the most technically advanced auto racing, where cars are designed like jet planes and run at a speed of more than 200 miles per hour. Formula refers to a certain set of rules all participants and cars should follow. The racing happens between closed circuits that are built and designed especially for a series of races called Grand Prix. The most famous Grand Prix is Monaco Grand Prix held in Monte Carlo. The first Grand Prix was held in 1950.

Sebastian Vettel is the youngest (21 years) and Luigi Fagioli (53 Years) is the oldest player to have won a Grand Prix.

361. Do you know that Michael Schumacher was a racer right at the age of 6?

Michael Schumacher, the F1 World Champion, holds the remarkable record for maximum Grand Prix victories, which is 91 times! Unbelievable, isn't it?

He was born in Germany. His mother ran a canteen while his father was a bricklayer who ran a local kart track. He then had the track available to him and he made the most out of it. He began to go-karting when he was just 4! By 6, he had won his first kart race!

He is known for his smooth driving skill, his instincts and the ability to go around the 'sharp curves' on the racing track. His biggest fear was to drive in wet conditions but he overcame his fear. Michael announced his retirement in 2006. But he returned in 2010 and finally retired in 2012.

362. Where were the first Olympics held?

No one is certain of the exact date and year but the Olympics games began about 2,700 years ago in Olympia, Greece. The games were part of a religious ceremony and were held in honour of Zeus, king of the gods every four years. It is believed that the Greek suspended their wars during the Olympics. These ancient Olympics included racing, boxing, wrestling, chariot racing, long jump, javelin and discus throwing.

A French man called Charles Pierre de Frédy revived these games. He was a very passionate sportsman and believed that sports can bring the world together and encourage peace. He travelled around the world with this message. Thanks to his determination, the first modern Olympic Games were held in Athens in 1896. Today Olympics is the most prestigious sports event where hundreds of nations compete in various games. Even, Paralympics have begun where people with disabilities participate in various sports.

The games are held in different countries every time. Prior to each game, the Olympic Torch or Flame is lit in Olympia, Greece and brought to the host city by runners carrying the torch in the relay.

363. Which cricketer is titled 'God of Cricket'?

Sachin Tendulkar of India is popularly titled as 'God of Cricket'. He holds the record of highest runs in one day cricket. He has scored 18,426 runs in 452 innings from 1989-2012. He is also the only player to have scored a double century (200 runs) in a One Day International (ODI) match.

Sachin Tendulkar began playing cricket at the age of 11 and made his debut in international test cricket against Pakistan at the age of 16! Sachin Tendulkar would practice for hours in the mornings and evenings. Sometimes when he got tired, his coach Achrekar would put a coin on the stumps. If anybody could bowl Sachin out, he would get the coin. And if Sachin could save himself, he would get the coin. According to Sachin, 13 coins he collected are his most prized possession. Sachin Tendulkar is considered to be the greatest batsman of the modern generation. He was declared the 'Wisden Cricketer of the Year' in 1997.

364. Which player is known as 'The Phenomenon' in football?

Ronaldo Nazario de Lima has scored the most goals in the FIFA World Cup. Ronaldo who is a player of the Brazilian team has scored fifteen goals in the FIFA World Cup. He was a celebrated striker and is fondly called 'The Phenomenon'!

At the age of 17, he was a part of the Brazilian team that won the 1994 FIFA World Cup. At the 1998 World Cup, he helped Brazil reach the final and won the Golden Ball for the player of the tournament. He won a second World Cup in 2002 where he received the Golden Boot as the top goal scorer. During the 2006 FIFA World Cup, Ronaldo became the highest goal scorer in World Cup history with his fifteenth goal. He retired from professional football in 2011.

FIFA (Fédération Internationale de Football Association) is one of the most viewed sporting events. Currently, 32 teams compete for the world cup. It is played every 4 years. The first world cup was held in 1930. The only years after that it was not organised were 1942 and 1946 due to the Second World War. Brazil has won FIFA World Cup 5 times! It is also the only nation that has played all the 19 FIFA World Cups.

365. When was the first Wimbledon event held?

The first Wimbledon event was held in 1877. It was actually held in a croquet lawn of a club called All England Croquet and Lawn Tennis Club. This was held only for men. It was only in 1884 that an even for women was also introduced. It was originally played by amateurs and was opened to professional players only in 1968.

Among the four Grand Slam tennis events, Wimbledon is the only one played on grass. The other Grand Slams are held in Australia, the US (hard court) and France (clay court).